AUTOBIOGRAPHY OF THE BLESSED MOTHER ANNE OF SAINT BARTHOLOMEW

INSEPARABLE COMPANION OF SAINT TERESA, AND FOUNDRESS OF THE CARMELS OF PONTOISE, TOURS AND ANTWERP : FRENCH TRANSLATION OF THE UN-PUBLISHED AUTOGRAPH OF THE VENERABLE SERVANT OF GOD, PRESERVED BY THE CARMELITES OF ANT-WERP, WITH COMMENTARY AND HISTORICAL NOTES. BY REV. MARCEL BOUIX, S.J. : TRANSLATED FROM THE FRENCH BY A RELIGIOUS OF THE CARMEL OF ST. LOUIS, MO., U. S. A.

Imprimatur

† JOANNES JOSEPHUS,
Archiepiscopus, Sti. Ludovici.

STI. LUDOVICI, *die 20 December, 1916.*

CONTENTS

AUTOBIOGRAPHY

FIRST BOOK

SECOND BOOK

Contents

THIRD BOOK

FOURTH BOOK

THE HOLY FATHER POPE BENEDICT XV'S REPLY

On the Reading of the Decree of Approval of Two Miracles, Wrought
by God Through the Intercession of the Venerable Servant of God,
Sister Anne of St. Bartholomew, Professed Nun of the Discalced
Carmelites, Sunday, February 25th, 1917.

"From our heart we join in the happiness which the Carmelite
Order feels at the solemn approval of two miracles wrought by
God through the intercession of the Venerable Anne of St. Bartholomew, and we are moved to do so by reasons both personal
to ourselves and inherent in our dignity.

"We will not stay to call to mind the ties which in our earliest
years and in our loved native place united us to illustrious members of the Teresian Order: the more than ordinary esteem which
we hold for that Order would be enough, even by itself, to make
us share in the joy just expressed in the name of all the members
of the deserving Order by its worthy head. But how can we help
saying how, while we can never at any time forget, today the
memory comes back to us, bringing us keener pleasure, of a visit
we paid to the convent at Alba di Tormes at the time when our
stay in Spain was drawing to its close? Fresh with us today as
if it had taken place yesterday, though indeed it is thirty years
ago, is the recollection of the tender emotion we felt before the
precious relic of the transverberated heart of St. Teresa. Ah, those
thorns which so suddenly appeared in a most unhappy hour for
the Church bear indeed the message that the spirit of the great
Reformer of Carmel is ever a-wing amid the Christian people and
thus shares their joys as well as their sorrows. But we think that
around that precious relic, together with the thorns—symbol of
the never-ceasing sorrows of the Church—little flowers should
grow, too, today, to witness the pleasure of St. Teresa in seeing
her faithful companion, Sister Anne of St. Bartholomew, so soon
to receive the cult of Blessed. And shall not the daughters of
St. Teresa, who, to kindle our interest in their Order, have so often
reminded us of our visit to the sepulcher of their Blessed Mother,
join us and all the children of the Reform of Carmel in thanking
the Lord for having used our littleness to hasten the honor of the
Blessed for their Sister?

FRESH INCREASE IN THE ORDER

"But, far more than for personal reasons, our share in today's
happiness of the Reformed Order of the Blessed Virgin of Mount
Carmel is grounded on reasons intimately connected with the high
dignity with which, without merit of our own, we are clothed.
Indeed, the care which, on account of our high ministry, we must
have for the well-being of the flock entrusted to us, brings to our

Address of His Holiness

heart the desire that the well-deserving institutes of the Christian people may spread ever more and more. To reach this desirable end, what is needed is a more widely diffused knowledge of the merits of those institutes. But are not the miracles wrought by God, at the intercession of His faithful servant, the seal which God Himself sets on the virtues of this privileged servant? And the wonders which God works through the intercession of a member of a certain family, or child of a certain religious Order, are they not a clear sign of the favor with which again God regards that Order or that family? We have reason, then, to draw the happiest auspices for a fresh and greater increase of the Carmelite Order from today's approval of the two miracles attributed to the intercession of the Venerable Anne of St. Bartholomew. Many souls thirsting for Christian perfection will follow the fragrance of the sweet-smelling flower reared in the mystic gardens of Carmel, and the Christian people will thus benefit from the new examples of virtues which will rejoice the earth, as from the new voices raised in heaven in prayer for them.

"And should not to your hymn be added perhaps the harmonious note of all who, in the increase of a religious Order, do not see merely an exclusive interest of its children? Should not they see, perhaps, full reason for the joy of all who, like the Pontiff, must be anxious for the good, not so much of some members, as of the whole mystical Body of Jesus Christ? But, without entering now, for lack of time, into the advantage of the whole Church in the multiplication of monastic Orders, suffice it to say that the joy we feel today is indeed caused by the well-founded hope that the renewed and more widespread knowledge of the Teresian Order may be fruitful of good, not only for a few individuals, but indeed for all the Christian people.

"THE SERAPH OF CARMEL"

"It is enough for the purpose to think of the very nature of the Carmelite Institute. Who does not see in that 'spirit of prayer' which gained for St. Teresa throughout the centuries the name of 'Seraph of Carmel,' and by which she wished her children to be guided, how she herself was ever informed by it even in the midst of troubles and the difficulties of her many 'foundations'? This spirit of prayer was learned directly at the school of the holy Mother by Sister Anne of St. Bartholomew, her inseparable companion for fourteen long years, sharing her most intimate confidences, receiving her last breath. And how surely and profoundly Sister Anne of St. Bartholomew learned from her holy Mother to express in herself the true character of the Carmelite Order is well shown by the marks of kindly deference which, after the death of St. Teresa, it was at once desired should be bestowed on her, first in Spain, then in the Gauls and Flanders. To the blessed Mother who wished to change her white veil to black, she had at first opposed sweet violence, founded on reasons of sound

Address of His Holiness

humility, but she could not persist in her opposition when she was elected mistress of novices—so clear and eloquent appeared in her the spirit of the holy Foundress. And shall we not say that with today's approval of two miracles wrought through the intercession of the Venerable Anne of St. Bartholomew, the Lord wishes to call the world again to that spirit of prayer which the happy daughter of St. Teresa drew with such living strength from her holy Mother?

AN OPPORTUNE CALL

"There is none but must see how opportune, indeed necessary, such a call is in our day. By the theories in vogue today, by the scandals which poison the world, by the very atmosphere in which they live, men of our age are miserably drawn towards the earth; to bear them to regions of purer air is a work of true compassion; and should not we rejoice in seeing this work of compassion wrought by God through today's recognition of two miracles attributed to the intercession of the Venerable Anne of St. Bartholomew? The record of the noble Order to which she belongs— she of whom the Lord availed Himself to carry out two perfect and instantaneous cures of diseases judged incurable—revives in us the thought of the spirit of prayer; indeed, should inspire in us a love for the spirit of prayer.

THE SPIRIT OF PRAYER

"Someone might say, perhaps, that that is the proper thought for monks and nuns, but that it is difficult to see the advantage to be drawn from it for the majority of men and especially those who, in the whirlwind of the times, live the troubled life of business, commerce and industry. But, of the two miracles approved today by the authority of the Church, while one rejoiced in a cloister the other brought happiness to a royal court; if the favored object of one was a minister of the sanctuary, it was a Queen of France who drew from the other benefits and life itself. The Lord does nothing by chance, and why should we not say that also under the gilded roof of a royal court was shown the efficacy of the intercession of the Venerable Anne of St. Bartholomew, because the Lord willed that men should know that the spirit of prayer was necessary for the life of the Christian, not only in convents and cloisters, but always and everywhere? This divine lesson has been repeated again today in the decree which recognizes the miracles wrought by God, both in a poor convent of Antwerp and in a rich palace of Ghent, through the intercession of her who, following in the footsteps of her great mistress, promoted and spread the spirit of prayer. We are justified, then, in sharing in the joy which the Carmelite Order feels today; evident is the good which all the Christian people can draw from the publication of the decree on the miracles attributed to the intercession of the Venerable Anne of St. Bartholomew.

Address of His Holiness

"Assuredly there is not one among you, beloved children, who thinks that the spirit of prayer imposes the obligation of continued or too frequent vocal prayers; you know that it consists principally in the uniting of the soul with God, and no one is ignorant that such union is wrought with the thoughts of the mind and the affections of the heart. But, that no empty or reasonless obstacle may prevent the spread of the spirit of prayer, do you, who know its fruits, spread it ever more, bring others to appreciate it. Say that it does not in the least tend to take us from our studies or occupations, but only claims to sanctify both the one and the other, directing all our work to the glory of God; say that as the dove, in order not to lose the whiteness of its wings, must always rise in flight without touching the mud of earth, so also, to keep pure, the Christian soul must live in a region where the pestilential breath of the age does not reach; and what is there better than the spirit of prayer to prevent the poisonous vapors of the earth reaching even the regions of the soul?

"Your exhortations and examples, beloved children, will succeed in spreading the divine lesson even in hearts which seem the least open to receive it. But, above all other benefits, will be the Benediction of the Lord, who, with loving counsel of providence towards us, has kept for our time the public recognition of the miracles wrought by Him, in days now long past, through the intercession of the Venerable Mother Anne of St. Bartholomew. And this Divine Benediction we invoke in copious measure on the illustrious Order to which the Venerable belonged; on Spain, which gave her birth; on Belgium, her country of adoption; on those who have striven to hasten the honor of the altars; and specially on all who have the intention to profit by her example and patronage to bring about that the Christians of our age all rule themselves by the true spirit of prayer."

J. M.

BROTHER CLEMENT OF STS. FAUSTINUS AND JOVITA,

Praepositus General of the Discalced Brethren of the Order of
B. V. M. of Mt. Carmel and Prior of the same Holy Mount.

To Our Beloved in Christ, the Fathers, Brothers, and Sisters of
Our Order, Greeting Everlasting in Our Lord:
"Blessed be the God and Father of our Lord Jesus Christ, the
Father of mercies and the God of all comfort," who, in the midst
of the many great sorrows and trials by which we are oppressed
in these dreadful times, has deigned to grant us a very great solace
and joy. For, on the 6th day of May of the present year, our
Most Holy Sovereign, Pope Benedict XV, will bestow the honors
of the Blessed in Heaven on Venerable Anne of St. Bartholomew,
that shining ornament of our Order, by enrolling her in the number of the beatified.

Hence our joy; hence our voice of exultation; for all of you
know in what esteem this virgin ought to be held, and with what
filial respect she ought to be venerated. She was an intimate and
familiar companion of our Holy Mother Teresa of Jesus, whom
she served up to her dying hour; and she inherited in a marked
degree her twofold seraphic spirit, namely, love and zeal for the
glory of God and for the salvation of souls.

There is no need of explaining how much this most happy
event redounds to the glory of God and our own advancement;
by it God's glory is increased—for whatever honor is bestowed
upon the Blessed and friends of God, all conduces to His glory—
and also a new model of excellent virtues is placed before us, and
a most powerful advocate with the Almighty is given to us, who,
in union with the Blessed of our Order, will procure more effica-
cious graces by which we may imitate her in this life and one day
become the sharers of her everlasting blessedness in heaven.

While, then, we announce to you the most joyful news of this
solemn event, we likewise exhort you to render due thanks to God
for this great favor. "Thanks be to God for this unspeakable
gift," especially during the solemn rites which are to be celebrated
with the greatest spiritual joy in all our churches throughout the
world on the day of the Beatification; since this is only fitting.

In view of the trying want in our communities and the affliction of the times, we should not dare to ask anything else; nevertheless, since our Very Reverend Father Postulator has to cover
the great expense of the cause of this Beatification, we should
like to suggest that every convent or monastery, as far as it is
able, generously contribute some alms, however small, for the
love of God and our Beatified Sister. And this will be the more

ix

Letter from Carmelite General

acceptable and will be the more liberally rewarded by God in proportion as it is given in a generous spirit.

Pray for us; and the peace and joy of the Holy Ghost be ever in your hearts.

Rome, the General's House, February 25, 1917.

BROTHER CLEMENT
OF STS. FAUSTINUS AND JOVITUS,
Praepositus General.

(L. S.)   BROTHER ELIAS OF ST. AMBROSE,
Secretary.

N. B.—Alms may be sent to our Very Reverend Father Postulator: Molto Reverendo Padre Rodrigo di S. Francesco di Paolo, Postluatore dei Carmelitani Scalsi, S. Maria della Vittoria, Roma (Italia).

DECREE

Referring to Antwerp and Malines, concerning the Beatification and Canonization of the Venerable Servant of God, Sister Anne of St. Bartholomew, professed Nun of the Order of Discalced Carmelites, in regard to the query: Whether there have been any miracles in the case, what kind they were, and whether they tend to the result of which there is question?

Whoever wishes rightly to know who Sister Anne of St. Bartholomew was, and with what great and splendid virtues she was adorned, cannot be better informed than by the famous Virgin of Avila, St. Teresa. For Sister Anne was her most beloved and inseparable companion, the sharer in her plans, the co-worker in her undertakings.

Hence it is that, since the one cannot easily be separated from the other, this apostolic decree, though it has reference to the disciple and daughter in the spiritual life, at the same time seems in some way to pertain to the mother and mistress and framer of the Rule. Among the Saint's far-famed sayings, sayings full of heavenly wisdom, this one stands out prominently: "God alone is enough and more than enough." This saying is most apropos in our own times because it goes down to the root of the numberless evils of our day, its bitter trials, its desolation and carnage. For by the rejection and neglect of the principles of the supernatural order and of Christian life, the greatest bulwark of justice has been taken away. Little wonder, then, if the human mind, filled with the poison of perverse opinions, should see itself and everything shrouded in darkness, after it has once departed from the right road.

Christ Jesus, who repaired the fault of humankind, well knew whilst on earth how to adapt the remedies most suitable to His times. Now, too, He so directed the course of events that the two cures here mentioned—one a cerebral disorder, the other a troublesome intestinal disease—have been rescued from the oblivion of the two or three centuries which have elapsed since their occurrence and are now become known and confirmed in the light of modern medical science, as if to show that error must first be rejected and the mind made sound in order that life may pulsate through the entire body.

Indeed, the proofs on which both occurrences rest, far from becoming old with the progress of time or being affected by corroding rust, have remained the same as they were when they were first judicially examined. For scarcely three or five years had elapsed since the two cures had occurred at the intercession with God of His faithful servant, Venerable Anne of St. Bartholomew. It was right, then, that the testimony of eye-witnesses should be

Decree for Beatification

heard and weighed, among them that of the two who were cured, Father Leopold and the Queen of France, as well as the depositions of physicians and others who saw with their own eyes the cures take place. Proofs were gathered at an opportune time from this source in full accordance with the law regarding inquiry into miracles and were preserved at that time and are still on hand. Moreover, from the series of judicial acts and the authority of illustrious men, skilled in their profession, which are contained in these proofs, it is clear that there was question of a true miracle in both cases.

They, indeed, not only by their extrinsic testimony, but also by means of weighty and persuasive arguments, tried especially to show that the diseases which had attacked Father Leopold and the Queen of France consisted in some organic or, as they call it, anatomical and pathological lesion. When they had, as it were, laid this foundation, the same experienced men then proceeded to inquire into and consider the manner in which the disease was entirely removed, both in the case of Father Leopold and the Queen of France, as it is described in the acts, and when they found out for certain that the cure had been sudden or instantaneous and perfect, they could not but immediately acknowledge and openly confess that these two wonderful cures transcended the powers of nature.

Nothing is more correct or more manifest than the judgment of these men, skilled as they were in their art. One need not be a philosopher or a doctor or a surgeon or an expert in other physical sciences to reach that same conclusion; for this, ordinary common sense is sufficient. Moreover, any man of the people, taught by the experience of daily life where he has never seen nor ever could see a serious and chronic malady, though not of itself incurable, fully and completely removed in a moment of time, with all accompanying injuries repaired, and so repaired that they seemed never to have existed, would, if such an event were to occur, be immediately filled with the greatest wonder, be overcome with amazement, and be forced in an irresistible way to cry out, perhaps even against his will, "This is a miracle!"

In order that all, even those ignorant of medical science, might easily and plainly see the truth of both of these miracles, a long, severe and exact discussion was held about the matter, first in the ante-preparatory Congregation, then in two subsequent preparatory Congregations, and lastly in a General Congregation, held on the 30th day of last January, in the presence of our Most Holy Father Pope Benedict XV. In this Congregation, the Most Reverend Cardinal Antonio Vico, the relator of the cause, proposed the following question for discussion: "Have there been any miracles in the case, what kind were they, and do they tend to the result of which there is question?" The Most Reverend Cardinals and Fathers Consultors voted one by one in order; but Our Holy Father, according to custom, postponed his supreme decision in

Decree for Beatification

order to give himself and those present time to implore help and illumination from the Father of Light.

On this first Sunday in Lent, however, after celebrating Mass most devoutly, he summoned the Most Reverend Cardinal Antonio Vico, Bishop of Portuensis and St. Rufina, Pro-Prefect of the Congregation of Rites, and relator of the cause, together with Reverend Father Angelo Maria, Promoter of the Faith, and myself, the undersigned Secretary, and in our presence solemnly declared that both are true miracles; namely, the first, the instantaneous and perfect cure of a chronic cerebral abscess, accompanied by symptoms of hyperemia and meningitis, in the case of Father Leopold of St. John the Baptist; and the second, the instantaneous and perfect cure of Mary, Queen of France, from prolonged typhoid fever, with immediate restoration of strength.

On the 25th day of February, 1917, he commanded that this decree become part of the public law and be placed in the acts of the Congregation of Sacred Rites.

ANTONIO, CARDINAL VICO,
Bishop of Portuensis and St. Rufina, Pro-Prefect of the Congregation of Sacred Rites.

(L. S.)   ALEXANDER VERDE, S.R.C.,
Secretary.

PREFACE

May God reward the Nuns of the Carmel of St. Louis for this translation of the life of Blessed Anne of St. Bartholomew, the first English version. It is a precious gift to the multitudes who otherwise would lack an entirely integral understanding of their beloved patroness, St. Teresa. The style is bright and lucid, the tone as fervent as Father Bouix's original. As to the subject-matter, it is, in every part, of absorbing interest. That "no man is great to his valet," has become a proverb. Not so when the great one is a Saint and the intimate associate is a saintly disciple.

The last twelve years of St. Teresa's life were stormy ones. From the foundation of her first monastery at Avila, amid a furiously militant antagonism, until she had founded her last monastery at Burgos, amid opposition peculiarly agonizing—six months before her death—this hero among religious founders was almost incessantly buffeted by enemies, some devilish, not a few pious but sadly misguided. And, although she had many hours of tranquil interior joy, yet there were just as many which paralleled the Apostle's state of soul: "Combats without, fears within." (II Cor., VII:5.)

Now the subject of this Life, this strong and beautiful soul, Sister Anne of St. Bartholomew, was St. Teresa's close companion during her later and most eventful years; indeed, so close to her in body and soul as to be a perfectly competent witness of not only all outward happenings, but also of many of her visions and revelations. Her narrative leads us to the fragrant borders of the Saint's paradise; this is Sister Anne's most precious gift. She was not an hour absent from the Holy Mother during six almost tragical months between the end of the Saint's Burgos foundation in the early Spring of 1582 and the seraphic end of her life the following October. Hence it is not too much to claim for this book that it is a necessary complement to St. Teresa's published writings; this is peculiarly true of her autobiography, which Sister Anne extends and completes to the Saint's expiring breath. Besides this unique excellence, the volume is a minute study at close hand of the holiness of Anne herself, who, simple lay-Sister though she was, was one of the best examples of the Saint's training of souls to Christian and religious perfection.

Between our Lord and St. John this is the inspired statement of relationship: "The disciple whom Jesus loved." (John XIX:26.) Much the same might be said of the union between St. Teresa and Sister Anne, to whom she prophesied two days before she died: "Daughter, the hour of my departure is coming." Anne tells us in this book that she never left St. Teresa's bedside after that except once. It was when the Father Confessor bade Anne

Preface

go and take some nourishment. Teresa missed her immediately; it was as if her angel had left her; she glanced from one face to another around the room as if searching for somebody. Anne presently returned, and the Saint's face lit up with joy, and she reached out for her. Then Teresa laid her head in Anne's arms. There it remained till she breathed her soul into the embrace of her Divine Spouse.

When Anne perceived that Teresa's death was near at hand, she longed and prayed that it might yet be delayed. And suddenly Christ appeared; the vision was granted for the Saint indeed, but Anne was privileged to share it with her. Our Savior appeared in great majesty, and many angels with Him. After a few minutes Teresa gently expired, and the vision faded away. Whilst it lasted Anne had prayed that the Saint's death might rather be hastened than delayed, for she had seen her eternal glory in God.

During the process for the Saint's canonization it was testified under oath, by the others who were present at the death scenes, that during Teresa's last moments Anne's face shone with such heavenly luster that in spite of themselves their eyes were drawn away from Teresa to gaze upon Anne, marveling that her face and form should reflect the dawning splendor of the Saint's eternal glory.

She had also been a plentiful partaker of Teresa's heavenly wisdom, receiving during the last era of her life not a few of her characteristic teachings. As Anne was the latest of her disciples, she was every way one of the most appreciative. It was her singular privilege to enjoy—all too painfully—her deepest confidence during the sorrowful journey from Burgos to Alba de Tormes, amid bodily perils of a peculiarly critical kind, and the shame of expulsion, as it must rightly be called, from the two Carmels of Valladolid and Medina del Campo, who owed their existence to her, and whose Sisters she had trained in the religious life—a lurid glare of bitterest penance preceding the bright twilight of her evening hours.

To know St. Teresa thoroughly well, one must have this Life of Sister Anne.

WALTER ELLIOTT, C.S.P.

PREFACE

The virgin whose life, written by herself, you are about to read, had a double mission to fill. God had chosen her first to be the inseparable companion of St. Teresa during the last years of her life, and afterwards to be one of the Foundresses of Carmel in France and Belgium.

Let us take a brief look at this double mission. It was the Divine Master Himself who prepared this virgin for the charitable ministrations she was to fulfill towards St. Teresa. He wished to be, Himself, her only Master and Guide until the moment when He would confide to her the charge and the care of the seraphic Teresa. The pages of the First Book of this Life present to us the ravishing picture of this spiritual education, where there was no intermediary between God and the soul. For the sanctification of the Reformer of Carmel, and that of her Coadjutrix in the work of the foundations, it pleased the Divine Master to associate with Himself two holy persons: to Teresa He gave, as guide, Father Balthasar Alvarez, and to Anne of Jesus, Father Pierre Rodriguez, S.J.; for seven years He left both under the guidance of these directors after His own heart. But for the sanctification of Anne of St. Bartholomew He wished to act alone, and He anticipated the usual time. Scarcely had this angelic creature reached the age of three years when He gave her the first lesson; He opened the heavens above her, and showed Himself to her, allowing a ray of His divinity to shine forth. The light she received at that moment regarding the greatness and sanctity of God remained present with her all her life. The Divine Master continued to instruct her; during her childhood He appeared to her in the form of a child, and as she advanced in age He seemed to grow with her. By His frequent apparitions He enkindled in this upright soul a love which never ceased to consume her. Properly speaking, He was always to be her guide; during the course of her long life, this privileged virgin was never to seek for interior direction but from the Master of her childhood and youth. Therefore, if Teresa and Anne of Jesus said in all justice and truth, "It was the company of Jesus that gave me life and being, that formed and trained me," Anne of St. Bartholomew could say with the same justice and truth: "It is the Chief Himself of this company who formed and trained me: *Me had criado y dado el ser.*"

To form an idea of the treasures of grace with which our Lord must have enriched this virgin, we must consider what St. Teresa was at the time when the Divine Master gave her Anne of St. Bartholomew as her inseparable companion. It was during the last years of the Reformer of Carmel. She was perfected in sanctity. Nearly fifteen years had passed since the cherub had pierced her

Preface

heart with his dart. She had heard from the mouth of the Divine Master these words—highest mark of His love in this life: "Henceforth, as My true spouse, you will care for My honor. *Deinceps ut vera sponsa, Meum zelabis honorem.*" This seraphic virgin, all burning, ascended from rapture to rapture in the fire of divine love. Most remarkable favors, most exalted visions, followed, and with these a prodigious increase in interior grace and charity. The state of her soul was that which she describes in the Sixth and Seventh Mansion of her Interior Castle; enjoying habitually in her soul the presence of our Lord and the intellectual vision of the Most Holy Trinity. Such was the height of sanctity to which St. Teresa had attained, when the Divine Master confided the care of her person to Anne of St. Bartholomew. To approach this Holy of Holies, this living tabernacle, it needed the purity of an angel and the love of a seraph. The Divine Master had engraven these two characteristics in her soul. Anne was one of the most angelic and seraphic virgins of her century. Not only the light of baptismal innocence shone in her with unalterable and ever-increasing brilliancy until her last sigh, but in her delightful uprightness and holy ignorance she did not, in some way, know the difference between herself and an angel, except for the advantage she had over an angel by being able to crucify her body and offer it to Jesus Christ as a holocaust of penance. From the time of her baptism until that of her entrance into heaven, her flesh, according to the beautiful expression of Tertullian, was angelic flesh—"*angelificata caro.*" As for the flames of divine love which consumed her heart, she has painted them herself in her life.

This is the one who was chosen and prepared by the Divine Master to be the inseparable companion and, as it were, visible angel of St. Teresa. She had the privilege of leaving her neither by day nor night, of lavishing her care upon her, preparing her food, washing her linen, and dressing her; for her arm, broken three times, refused her all service; in fine, taking care of all that concerned her person. She shared all the fatigues of her journeys and the labors of her last foundations, which were the most trying of all. When the pilgrimage of this great Saint was reaching its end, her inseparable companion showed herself more worthy than ever of the mission which she fulfilled towards her; the tenderness of her charity was shown in the most touching manner. During the journey from Burgos to Alba her heart was pierced by the sufferings which she beheld the seraphic Mother enduring. But during her last sickness at Alba, and, above all, from the time she learned from her own mouth that her last hour had come, she experienced a real interior agony at the thought of the separation. However, hiding this martyrdom, and unfailing in charity, she was on her feet night and day, never far from the Saint, and giving herself scarcely time to take, in passing, some mouthfuls of bread to sustain her.

Before the holy Mother entered into the ecstasy of fourteen hours, which was to anticipate for her the clear vision of God,

Preface

Anne hastened to prepare her for the eternal nuptials. Let us listen now to her own words: "The day on which she died I changed everything on her—linen, sleeves, headdress and tunic. She looked herself over completely, and was quite pleased to see how neat she was, and, turning her eyes towards me, she looked at me, smiling, making known by signs her gratitude. Thus the seraphic virgin was adorned to appear before her Spouse."

On the 4th of October, Feast of St. Francis of Assisi, at seven o'clock in the morning, having her dear companion beside her, she rested on her poor couch like a queen on her throne; supported in the arms of Anne of St. Bartholomew, her head resting on her heart, she entered into the highest ecstasy of her entire life; and after this prolonged foretaste of the Beatific Vision, it was from the arms of her companion that she finally took her flight to heaven.

Anne, virgin dearly beloved of Christ, how great thou art, and how touching in this scene! Thou holdest on thy heart Teresa, resplendent in glory, and thou givest her back to the Divine Spouse who comes to seek her with His saints and His angels. Thou hast become dear to the whole Church; and all those who will cherish filial devotion for the seraphic Teresa will love thee for all that thou hast done for her. Carmel, thy family, will cherish thee with the most tender blessings. But who can ever understand how Jesus Christ and Teresa will repay thee for this great work of charity! Be inundated with happiness, for, in return, neither one nor the other will ever again avert their looks from thee.

Anne of St. Bartholomew is known to us as the companion of St. Teresa. Let us consider her now as a Foundress.

For this second mission three qualities must be united in her: holiness, the spirit of her Order, authority. We will now see in how eminent a degree the Divine Master granted them to her.

As we have seen, He was, Himself, the guide of this angelic creature from the age of three years until her entrance into Carmel. As this soul possessed wonderful purity, she gained more and more the predilection of the Divine Master, and received from Him every day new treasures of grace. From the time of her entrance into Carmel until her departure for France, He continued to be her guide. During the ten years that He placed her in such intimate contact with St. Teresa it pleased Him to embrace these two souls together as one: Anne, near Teresa and under the guidance of the Divine Master, flew rather than walked in the ways of holiness. Gifted with the most signal favors, she responded by heroic fidelity; from this time there was no limit to the graces of the Divine Master nor to the munificence of His gifts. The ties were drawn closer and closer; the Adorable Master, who guarded her as the apple of His eye, no longer left her, assisted her always, and took a paternal care of her soul. One may judge to what sanctity she was raised.

As to the spirit of her Order, the Divine Master had placed the germ in her soul in her tenderest years; so much so that when she

Preface

entered Carmel it seemed to her that she had passed all her life there. But He completely developed this germ by making her the inseparable companion of St. Teresa. Anne, living in the most intimate manner with the Foundress, witness of her actions, enjoying her conversation, following her in her journeys and the foundation of her monasteries, drank in unceasingly the spirit of Carmel from the most pure and elevated source—I dare to say, from the heart even of the seraphic Teresa. After the Saint's death she lived in the monasteries she had founded and with her first daughters; and for twenty-two years she witnessed the Constitutions of Carmel applied and practised by them. Therefore, when in 1604 she arrived in France, she had observed this holy Institute during thirty-four years, in the company of St. Teresa as well as in that of her first daughters. As for the distinctive characteristic of this Order, that which is the soul of Carmel—I mean to say, apostolic zeal—the Divine Master had deeply engraved it in her. Her heart admirably resembled, in apostolic fervor, the heart of St. Teresa. She tells us, herself, in her Life, how far this flame consumed her in this world. With such sanctity, and so filled with the spirit of the Order, what must have been her authority when she appeared at the head of the monasteries in France! How must souls have been impressed by her title of "Companion of St. Teresa," her thirty-five years of religious life, virtues practised to a heroic degree, the extraordinary graces which the Divine Master unceasingly showered upon her, her high prayer, her ecstasies, her prophetic lights and the gift of miracles! What holy respect must not the ravishing modesty of this virgin have inspired, her truly angelic bearing, the unchanging serenity of her countenance, and the impress of the penance of half a century visible on her features! But, above all, what a sweet and irresistible ascendency was given her over souls by the love which God, at the most tender age, enkindled in her heart, and which had only increased during all those years. This Divine love shone forth in her looks and in her person. Finally the Divine Master gave her, as to Judith, a splendor of sanctity which made her all-powerful over hearts. This Adorable Master, who delighted in her, directed her in everything, instructed her, consoled her, encouraged her, and often favored her with His presence. St. Teresa, from the height of her glory, became in her turn the inseparable companion of the one who had so tenderly assisted her on earth; she lightened the burden of her charge; she exercised with her the office of Prioress; she made her, in some way, enjoy in France, as in Spain, the happiness of living in her holy company. We will hear Anne of St. Bartholomew telling us in the account of her Life: "It was the seraphic Mother who did all."

There is no cause for surprise at the prodigies which marked the career of Anne of St. Bartholomew as Foundress. The first monastery she founded was that of Pontoise. Let us listen to her speaking to us herself of the virgins she had formed to the religious life:

Preface

"Our Lord kept me in the Carmel of Pontoise as if in a heaven. It pained me, after having so long trained them, to separate myself from these souls, who seemed to be angels. The Divine Master did not allow them to touch the earth. He carried them, as it were, in His arms, so much consolation and spiritual joy did He lavish on them."

Such is the historical portrait of the Carmel of Pontoise left us by the Foundress. How interesting is the biography of these virgins! What an angelic spouse of Christ and how holy a character is that of Charlotte du Pucheul; so rich in treasures of grace from her most tender years as to call forth the admiration of St. Francis de Sales. What a heroine was Valence de Marillac, destined one day to see her father die in prison and her uncle perish on the scaffold, but obtaining for both the grace to make to God the sacrifice of their lives, with the faith and calmness of martyrs. Among the virgins who made the Carmel of Pontoise illustrious, the character which rises above all the others is that of the Blessed Mary of the Incarnation. She entered this retreat sanctified by Anne of St. Bartholomew, to spread abroad the last perfumes of her holy life. There, from the height of the altar where the Church has placed her, she will keep intact in this convent the traditions left by the companion of St. Teresa.

Tours, the city of St. Martin, was to have the glory of possessing a community of the daughters of St. Teresa. This was the second monastery founded by Anne of St. Bartholomew. God caused His prodigies to be manifested there. St. Teresa appeared to Anne of St. Bartholomew, when from Paris she turned her steps towards Touraine. She promised her her assistance. Carmel, though scarcely founded, shone with such brilliant sanctity that the heretics, who were numerous in the city, were not slow to send forth this cry of despair: "The Teresians will end by converting us all." From the very day of the foundation the Divine Master wished to manifest to His faithful servant how agreeable this new monastery was to Him, and made her the most consoling promises regarding those who were to occupy it during the course of centuries. But it is to the very words of Blessed Mother Anne of St. Bartholomew that we must listen now:

"The Sunday following the Ascension, the day on which the Most Blessed Sacrament was placed in the Monastery of Tours, while I was preparing for Communion, I asked our Lord that this beginning should be accomplished by His grace, and that with this grace He would deign to assist us who were present, and all who should come after until the end. Then my Adorable Master gave me positive assurance that He would do so, and that He granted my request."

Happy the community of daughters of St. Teresa, sheltered under the crosier and the tomb of the great St. Martin. Supported by such a promise from the Divine Master, with what courage they should combat and offer themselves in sacrifice for the salvation of souls.

Preface

This monastery of Tours soon gave forth such a perfume of
sanctity, and enjoyed so great renown throughout the entire country, that the most desirable subjects, the flower of the nobility,
came to place themselves under the guidance of Anne of St. Bartholomew. God blessed the direction of His servant. This convent was to be a centre from which light was to be spread abroad.
Several who shared the spirit of Anne of St. Bartholomew
were to leave the Carmel of Tours to found other monasteries.
The noble families of Quatrebarbes and of Montalembert were to
be represented in this Carmel, and it was Elizabeth de Quatrebarbes who was to leave Tours for Beaune to lead in the ways of
sanctity Margaret of the Blessed Sacrament, whom France is
striving today to place on the altar.

Anne of St. Bartholomew established the spiritual edifice with
which she gifted the City of St. Martin on such firm foundations
that the revolutionary tempest of the last century was unable to
make the least breach. One of the community was eighty-seven
years of age and deprived of sight; this was Venerable Mother
Amable: a victim of inhuman treatment, she rejoiced and had the
glory of dying in prison for the faith of Jesus Christ. Soon some
of their number were condemned to death. They were to be taken
to Issoudem, there to be shot. They exulted with celestial joy at
the prospect of martyrdom. They had started on their way, but
God, who had witnessed the preparation of their hearts, left them
the merit of martyrdom and delivered them miraculously from
the hands of their enemies. These virgins, rather angels, returned to Tours to make themselves prisoners with their Sisters.
In prison they kept living and intact the spirit of Carmel. And
when liberty was restored to Catholic worship, they lived, at first
scattered in the city, preserving inviolable obedience to their Prioress; and afterwards returning with delight to their former home.
The customs had not been interrupted; therefore, the beauty of
Carmel was seen to flourish again in the monastery as if it had
just come from the government of the Foundress. In the middle
of this century this convent full of the primitive sap has given to
the Church and the world Sister St. Pierre, whose life will furnish
one of the most attractive pages of the history of Carmel. She
appears there with her aureole of miraculous graces, holding in
her hand the banner of reparation. For it is to her the arch-con-
fraternity for the reparation of blasphemy and the violation of
Sunday owes its existence. The Perpetual Reparation founded
by Mlle. Dubouchet, and the Nocturnal Adoration, also owe her
their origin. Taken away at thirty-one years of age, this virgin
has left by her passage on earth a luminous track and imperish-
able monuments of her zeal.

It was at Antwerp that the apostolic work of Anne of St. Bartholomew was to finish; Antwerp was to be the crown of her
foundations. Teresa, by the hand of her companion, was to
plant her banner in this city; the pride of the Netherlands, the
metropolis of her commerce, of her printing-houses; celebrated

Preface

for its antiquity, for its great men; rich in so many religious wonders and illustrious souvenirs; the country of Rubens and Van Dyck, the cradle of the Bollandists, who by their *Acta Sanctorum* have given to their country a national glory that the rest of the world envies.

Even in Spain God had revealed to Anne of St. Bartholomew that she would only be seven years in France; and that the Netherlands would possess the last years of her life. While she was still at Tours our Lord showed her the house at Antwerp where she would soon go to found a new monastery, and the first novice she would receive.

On the 6th of October, 1611, she left Paris and proceeded to Mons, where she spent one year. There the Divine Master made known to her the mission she was to fulfill in these new states; He showed her the foundation at Antwerp, as a great torch, a resplendent light which was to shine through all the neighboring countries.

Encouraged by this revelation of the Divine Master, Anne of St. Bartholomew started forward without delay. She greeted, at Marimont, the Archduke Albert and the Infanta Clare Isabel-Eugenie, who had earnestly desired to see her and lavished upon her proofs of their veneration. She stopped several days at Brussels, where Anne of Jesus received her with open arms; it was a family feast. On the 29th of October, 1612, she left Brussels with the companions who had accompanied her from Mons. Arriving at Antwerp, she was received with honor by a son of St. Francis Borgia. Don Ignatius Borgia and Doña Helena, his wife, offered her hospitality in their palace. The entire city considered themselves happy in possessing her. Finally, on the 6th of November, 1612, the monastery was founded. St. Teresa, by means of her companion, took possession of the great Flemish city. What the Fathers of the Company of Jesus had done in Spain for St. Teresa in her foundations, the Jesuits of Antwerp did for Anne of St. Bartholomew; the same willingness for all sorts of good offices.

On the 21st of November, Feast of the Presentation of the Blessed Virgin, the first novice, Mlle. de Dompre, whom the Divine Master had shown her in a vision in France, received from Mother Anne the holy habit; the Archbishop of Cambrai, her uncle, performed the ceremony; and Anne of St. Bartholomew gave her the beautiful name of Teresa of Jesus.

Among the most noble benefactresses of this monastery was the Duchess of Bournonville, one of the many Christian women of her century. She had so high an esteem of the holiness of Mother Anne of St. Bartholomew that, in order to enjoy seeing her, and profit by her conversations and counsels, she obtained from the Pope permission to enter the monastery six times a year with her daughters. It was during one of these visits that the holy Foundress, looking tenderly at the little Anne-Eugenie de Bournonville, said to the duchess: "Madam, this one will some day

Preface

be my daughter." In 1643, seventeen years after the death of the servant of God, her prophecy was verified; Mlle. Anne-Eugenie de Bournonville took, at the Carmel of Antwerp, together with the holy habit, the name of Anne-Eugenie of St. Bartholomew. Later she governed this monastery; and she was the first to write its Annals.

In 1657 the Duchess of Bournonville, after the death of the duke, her spouse, took the holy habit at the age of sixty-six years. And, as still can be seen to-day by the formula of her profession, signed by her own hand and preserved at the Carmel of Antwerp, the Princess d'Epinay, granddaughter of the Montmorency, the Duchess of Bournonville, giving up all her titles, made it her highest ambition to be called Sister Anne-Francis of St. Joseph. Finally, in 1660, full of days and merit, she finished her life in sanctity. Her daughter closed her eyes, and leaves us her historical portrait.

The fourteen last years of the life of Anne of St. Bartholomew were passed at Antwerp. The Carmelites she formed were worthy of such a mistress of the spiritual life. St. Teresa was pleased with this monastery, which was a true copy of St. Joseph of Avila. The servant of God was there as if in a paradise of grace. The pages she has written about this part of her life show us with what an abundance of gifts and with what tender love the Divine Master favored her. It was for her like a foretaste of the beatific life. Owing to the wonderful favors, visions and apparitions with which her Divine Spouse honored her, she lived less on the earth than in the abode of the blessed, so that it may be said that during the last part of her life she was raised with the flight of a seraph to that height of sanctity which was to place her in heaven near St. Teresa. The Divine Master was pleased to make these magnificent interior graces shine forth exteriorly. His faithful servant often appeared completely transfigured and as if crowned with rays of light in her raptures and ecstasies. A perfume of holiness emanated from her person, and the majesty of the living God, who was within her, gave her an august and dignified bearing. The gift of miracles and prophecy, added to this, caused her to be regarded as a Saint. Here is one of her prophetic lights:

One day, ravished in ecstasy, she was carried in spirit to the college of the Company of Jesus. There she witnessed the wondrously beautiful death of Father John Chailant. He was a religious renowned for sanctity, with whom the Blessed Mother had been intimate, from whom her soul derived the greatest consolation. She saw him seated in his cell, his hands raised to heaven and his face radiant. She then appeared to him. The happy son of St. Ignatius looked at her and said: "St. John the Evangelist has just been here, and has brought me good news, such that none better could be wished for: it is that I am to depart this very hour for heaven." Having said these words, his soul went to be immediately united with God. It was discovered that the holy religious expired at the very hour when the Blessed

Preface

Mother was in ecstasy, and in the position in which she had beheld him.

He who exalts the humble delighted to glorify her in the eyes of the Church. Her power with God was known not only in the Netherlands, but also throughout all Europe. The great ones of the earth, princes and kings, recommended themselves to her. The immortal daughter of Philip II, the Infanta Clare-Isabel Eugenie, who governed the Netherlands, esteemed her as a Saint already canonized. With what faith this illustrious princess, bending the knee before her, kissed her hand, and asked her blessing. She consulted her on all important affairs, often wrote to her with her own hand, and was intimate with her. When she left for Breda, stopping at Antwerp, she wished to enter the convent three times to see the Blessed Mother, and remained several hours with her, thus showing the faith and devotion she had in her prayers. Bidding her good-bye, she begged her blessing. She wished, moreover, at the door of the convent, that the holy Prioress should bless all the grandees of the court, that no evil should molest them in the expedition to Breda. She said to them, therefore, in a loud voice: "Receive the blessing of Mother Anne of St. Bartholomew, who will be your assurance and safeguard against every peril."

With knees bent to the ground and heads inclined, they received it with this firm belief, and a few days later Breda was in the hands of the Infanta.

The faith of this princess in the sanctity and power of Anne of St. Bartholomew, with God, was shown in the reply she made to one of her subjects who advised her to fortify the citadel and town of Antwerp: "I do not fear either for the town or the citadel since Mother Anne of St. Bartholomew is there: she is a stronger defense than all armies united. "

So noble and entire a confidence was justified in a most striking manner. Twice the holy guardian of Antwerp delivered the city from the invasion of the Hollanders. It was this merited for her the glorious title of Deliverer of Antwerp. It was in this great city that the term of her pilgrimage closed. On the 7th of June, 1626, Feast of the Most Holy Trinity, this seraphic spouse of the God of virgins left her exile in the seventy-sixth year of her age and took flight to her heavenly country. The last moments of this well-beloved of the Lord, as will be seen at the end of this work, presents one of the most majestic and touching scenes that the eye of a Christian could contemplate. Her funeral was a real triumph. Every great one in the Netherlands was either present in person or represented by another. The inhabitants of Antwerp surrounded this coffin as of one who was a Mother, a Saint, their protectress in heaven. Thus this *Labradorcilla*, this humble shepherdess, received honors which surpassed those that would be given to the daughter of a king. It was because they discovered in her still higher titles: in this humble virgin Faith bowed before the heroic and seraphic spouse of Christ. To the eyes of faith, her white mantle was the royal mantle of sanctity; the linen that

Preface

bound her forehead was the diadem of a virgin seated in glory next to the King of Kings. This is why they could not tire of looking upon her, lavishing upon her marks of veneration, and recommending themselves to her influence with God. She was thus glorified, because in the Church she was a column by her faith, a torch by her sanctity, and one of the most apostolic women of her century by the greatness of her zeal. The miracles which took place, after her last sigh, attest the glory she enjoys with God; and these miracles have continued up to our own days. A century after her death, the 29th of June, 1735, Pope Clement XII proclaimed, by a solemn decree, the heroicity of her virtues. In these later times steps have been taken for her beatification. But the moment marked by God has not yet come; the infinite wisdom of God has not, perhaps, found minds disposed to receive the blessing of her beatification.

Towards the end of the last century Madam Louise de France, Prioress of the Carmel of St. Denis, writing to Pope Pius VI, recommended to him with most filial earnestness the causes of Mary of the Incarnation, Anne of Jesus, and Anne of St. Bartholomew, wishing to see all three raised to the altar. Pius VI made this reply: "We recognize more and more how the interests of religion touch you, and that you live only for the glory of God. We will beg of Him to guide us by His spirit of counsel and wisdom to do that which He wills of us for His glory, for, you know full well, the issue of an affair of such consequence to the Church is not in the power of any human will."

No; canonization is not in the power of any human will. Of the three servants of God named above, one only, Mary of the Incarnation, was placed in the ranks of the Blessed by Pius VI, the 10th of April, 1791. God willed that the Carmel of France should be the first to be glorified, and that the first Blessed of the Order, after St. Teresa, should be a French Carmelite. God proved by this that the Carmel of France, with the style of government given it by the Holy See, possesses as much as any Carmel of the world the conditions necessary for leading souls to sanctity.

As for the venerable servants of God, Anne of Jesus and Anne of St. Bartholomew, Pius VI thought right to await new lights before placing them on the altar. Let us hope that his successors will, in the near future, accede to the wishes of St. Teresa's children. May the Life that we publish hasten this happy moment.

It now remains for us to speak of the Autobiography of the Venerable Mother Anne of St. Bartholomew. What painter could ever have succeeded in portraying this figure? What historian could have found words to relate this life, miraculous from the cradle to the grave?

The Divine Master has overcome all difficulties: He has done for Anne of St. Bartholomew what He did for St. Teresa. Wishing that the extraordinary graces with which He had endowed these two virgins should be known in His Church, He placed the pen in their hands and ordered them to write; He willed that their

Preface

portraits should be drawn by themselves, in order that they might
be the faithful expression of the sanctity and celestial beauty of
their souls. Anne has, therefore, obeyed like Teresa; she has
written her own Life; this book still exists in manuscript, reli-
giously preserved at the Carmel of Antwerp, where it was composed. It is the real life, the interior life, of the Venerable Servant
of God, the recital of the graces and mercies she received from
God from the time of her most tender childhood at Almendral,
the place of her birth, until her last years at Antwerp, where she
finished her career.

This precious treasure has been preserved until this day; these
pages in the Castilian language, written by this great servant of
God, have never been printed. It is this unpublished work, so
full of heavenly unction, that we offer today to the public, and
in particular to the daughters of St. Teresa.

The precious autograph, which seems to have been written but
yesterday so admirably is it preserved, was placed in our hands
by the Carmel of Antwerp; and it is this autograph that we
translate.

Our Commentary and Historical Notes accompany the text of
the Venerable Servant of God. Among other sources we draw from
the Manuscript Chronicles of the Convents she founded. This
Life will be one of the complements of our works on St. Teresa.*

From the beginning, the present work entered into the plan
we proposed to ourselves. We wished to offer this homage to
St. Teresa, certain that it would be accepted by her. Therefore,
the thought of this publication came entirely from us and our
devotion to St. Teresa and her inseparable companion. But, as
soon as we had made known our intention to the Carmels founded
by the Venerable Mother Anne of St. Bartholomew, this idea was
greeted with all the transports of filial piety; they showed a noble
ambition to aid us, and their archives were placed at our disposal.
The Monastery of Antwerp, the most privileged of all, because
it held the body of the Venerable Anne, and possessed besides the
autograph of her Life, her other writings and a great number of
letters, offered us all the assistance we could desire. The Prioress
of this convent, a descendant of the illustrious house Della Faille,
with the exquisite courtesy due to her birth and to which the title
of Daughter of St. Teresa had added a peculiar distinction, confided to us the autographs and the manuscripts of the Annals of
her convent. Then, too, on different occasions, she has assured
us, both in speaking and by letters, in her own name as well as
in that of her daughters, that after the works of St. Teresa and
her Life by Ribera, the monument raised to the glory of Anne

---

* We consider four works as the complement to our works on St.
Teresa: Her Life, by Ribera; the Life of Father Balthasar Alvarez, her
director; the Life of the Venerable Mother Anne of Jesus, her coadjutrix
in the work of the foundations; and the Life of Venerable Mother Anne of
St. Bartholomew. God grant us strength to publish the others.

Preface

of St. Bartholomew would be one of the greatest consolations to their souls in this life.

It was in the same spirit and with the same nobility, we must in truth acknowledge, that the Reverend Mother Prioress of the Carmel of Tours constantly expressed herself regarding this family publication; and here she interpreted the well known sentiments of the Carmel of France. Our work will present particularly the narrative of the graces and mercies of our Lord towards the inseparable companion of St. Teresa. And this choice would seem, beyond all doubt, far preferable to details or questions regarding Mother Anne's rule and government of monasteries. It will be seen that our constant object has been to edify, console and encourage souls consecrated to the highest perfection, and particularly the daughters of St. Teresa.

We will close this preface with a few words regarding the persecution which assailed the Monastery of Antwerp towards the end of the last century, and the providential preservation of the remains of the Venerable Mother Anne of St. Bartholomew.

Until the year 1782 the Carmel of Antwerp was prosperous, and the bones of its holy Foundress rested in peace. But in 1783 this monastery was submitted to the most serious trials, and the virginal remains of Anne of St. Bartholomew, taken from the tomb, must journey into exile. The author of this persecution was the Emperor Joseph II. This prince, raised by a man, a slave to the heresy of Jansenism, had learned from his preceptor that the right and duty of a monarch was to govern the Church in his kingdom. Imbued with such perverse maxims, Joseph II posed as an autocrat, and as a despotic oppressor of the Church. He overwhelmed with sorrow the immortal Pontiff Pius VI, whose authority and paternal remonstrances he disdained; he published a series of edicts tending to annihilate the rights of the Church and the Holy See. Alas! he did not realize, in the delirium of his sacrilegious despotism, that by such acts he bequeathed to the inheritors of his scepter a joint responsibility that would draw down on them those terrible expiations written today in history as one of the greatest lessons God could give to sovereigns.

Among other fundamental deviations from Christian principles, and among other abuses of royal power, Joseph II became the persecutor of religious Orders, particularly of contemplative Orders. Under the pretext that they were useless and hurtful to States he suppressed a great number of these monasteries in Hungary as well as in Austrian Flanders, and confiscated their belongings for the benefit of the crown. The monasteries of the Carmelites of Brussels and Antwerp endured this fate. The Infanta Clare-Isabel Eugenie, who governed the Netherlands, had founded with royal magnificence the Convent of Brussels, and showered her gifts on that of Antwerp; she had shown by constant marks of her affection and respect that she fully understood how great and apostolic was the mission of the daughters of St. Teresa. Not the great memories connected with the origin of these two convents,

Preface

nor the authority of the name of the granddaughters of Charles V, nor the courageous protests of the Belgians, could protect them from the sentence of the philosophical and reforming monarch.

During the persecution of Joseph II, who expelled from their retreats so many virgins consecrated to Jesus Christ, a descendant of St. Louis, Madame Louise of France, who then made Carmel famous by the sanctity of her life, conceived the idea of offering them all a refuge in her country. She asked this favor of Louis XVI, her nephew; the future martyr king entered with joy into the project of the pious princess. Immediately Madame Louise sent word to all the virgins banished from their holy retreats, offering them a home in the convents of France. She addressed herself particularly to the daughters of St. Teresa, who were her sisters; and as she followed with the greatest zeal the cause of the canonization of Anne of Jesus and Anne of St. Bartholomew, she obtained permission from Pope Pius VI that the Carmelites who would come to her Convent of St. Denis should bring her the bodies of these two illustrious daughters of St. Teresa. On the 14th of June, 1783, the community of Brussels arrived at St. Denis with this double treasure.

The holy remains of the Foundresses of the Carmel of France were received with all transports of filial love and with all the respect inspired by faith. These two virgins came to crown their apostolate in the most Christian kingdom; they came to uplift and ennoble the hearts of the Carmelites of France, on the eve of the storms which threatened them.

Scarcely had four years passed when Madame Louise of France reached the end of her holy life. She had offered herself to God in Carmel, as a victim of expiation for her family and for France. Understanding all that was required of her by such a mission, she had walked with giant strides in the path of sanctity. In the ardor of the zeal which consumed her she had thousands of times given her life for God, for His Church, and for France. And though she had not shed her blood for Jesus Christ, the palm of martyrdom had not been wanting to her. What she had experienced in seeing Louis XV, her father, imprinting by his private life so many deplorable stains on the throne of St. Louis; what she had felt from the age of twenty-four, in witnessing him signing, through weakness, the suppression of the Company of Jesus, this was for her the sword of martyrdom and of wounds which will be known only in heaven. Thus God, who sees all, wished to cover with glory the last hours of this august victim. It might be said that He sent Anne of Jesus and Anne of St. Bartholomew to hold this noble virgin in their arms, like another Teresa, at the moment when she would take her flight from the Convent of St. Denis to her celestial country. The first ray of the glory of the blessed already shone upon her head; the heavens opened, Jesus Christ extended to her His arms. "Let us go;" she cried. "Let us rise up; let us hasten to enter Paradise."

Preface

The powerful intercession of Anne of Jesus and Anne of St. Bartholomew were to work other prodigies near their holy relics. A spiritual daughter of Madame Louise of France, a Carmelite of St. Denis, Madame de Chamboran, imbibed the fire of divine charity, and the strength of martyrdom. Led to the scaffold several years later, she made her confession: "I am a child of the Catholic Church." After these words, adorned with the blood of martyrdom, she went to join in heaven the daughter of St. Louis.

Animated with the same heroism, the Carmelites of Compiegne went to the scaffold singing hymns, and radiant as angels they gathered the palm of martyrdom. Happy virgins! With their Sisters of St. Denis, they bequeathed to the Carmel of France an eternal title of glory: first among all the daughters of St. Teresa, they shed their blood for Jesus Christ. And if, during the tortures of the Revolution, all the daughters of St. Teresa in France proved themselves angels of virtue before the world, one need not be astonished. Anne of Jesus and Anne of St. Bartholomew were interceding with God for this Carmel, which they have so deeply imbued with the spirit of the holy Foundress.

In 1790, the condition of Belgium permitting the daughters of St. Teresa to return to their convents, the Carmelites of Flanders who were in France started on their homeward journey, taking with them the holy bodies of Anne of Jesus and Anne of St. Bartholomew.

On the 11th of October of the same year the Carmelites re-entered their convent with great solemnity. The cell which Venerable Mother Anne of St. Bartholomew had occupied was converted into an oratory and her remains placed there. But it was, alas! a rest of only a few years. In 1796 the French Revolution suppressed their convent once more. They found themselves expelled during the month of July. Happily, in the month of May they had placed in safety the most precious of their treasures, the mortal remains of Anne of St. Bartholomew. One of the most honorable families of Antwerp had the immense honor of sheltering under its roof the shrine enclosing the body of the inseparable companion of St. Teresa. So great a privilege was the recompense of piety, long hereditary in this family. The holy shrine was guarded with all the devotion and respect that faith could inspire. As in olden times, during the persecution of emperors, the Christians kept hidden the bodies of the martyrs and regarded them as a more precious treasure than all the riches of the world; so the family, to whom the virginal body of Blessed Mother Anne of St. Bartholomew was confided, secreted it, showed it every mark of respect, and esteemed it above all the diamonds of this earth. The holy shrine was the wonder-worker of this family. It brought down upon them a stream of blessings which never ceased to flow. Anne of St. Bartholomew was pleased even to show, by the eloquent proof of a miracle, how the Saints and favorites of God repay the kindness of hospitality received. But here we consider it our duty to give place to the worthy son of

Preface

the one whose days the servant of God miraculously prolonged, Count Gerard Le Grelle. Happy the Christian who can bequeath to his descendants so touching a page in the family souvenirs.

"The remains of Anne of St. Bartholomew, enclosed in a leaden coffin, which covered a shrine of oak, was confided during the month of May of this year 1796 to the care of my parents, and the treasure was carefully hidden in a linen-closet, where it remained out of sight, under napkins and tablecloths, during the tempest of the Revolution. During this terrible time my parents' house was not molested, though unsworn priests were constantly sheltered, a chapel re-established there, daily Mass celebrated and Holy Communion given to quite a number of persons. It seemed as if Anne of St. Bartholomew, who was resting there, had taken it under her special protection. But the finger of God was shown in a still more striking way, when my father, taken with a very serious illness, was obliged to submit to a dangerous operation. On account of the late hour of the night it was postponed until the following day, and the last Sacraments had been ordered. My pious mother had recourse to the intercession of Venerable Mother Anne of St. Bartholomew, and passed part of the night in prayer before her relics. Suddenly, without any remedies, without the least effort, my father was completely cured. And when the physicians returned at break of day to the sick one they could not believe the sudden change which had taken place. 'What has happened here?' they cried out. 'This is astonishing! It is a prodigy!' My family could reveal nothing of the supernatural cause to which they attributed the unexpected cure of my father, as they were obliged to observe the most profound secrecy regarding the presence of the precious deposit, and my parents were forced to content themselves with thanking, silently, God and their powerful protectress.

"When, in 1801, the First Consul had restored to the Catholic religion part of its liberty, the Carmelites of Antwerp took advantage of it to return immediately to their former home, which a generous benefactor had purchased that it might be returned to them. Their first desire, on finding themselves in their monastery, was to have with them again the remains of their saintly Foundress. My parents therefore parted regretfully with the venerated treasure, which had brought them so many great favors, and preserved all their lives a particular devotion for Anne of St. Bartholomew."

The precious shrine was returned for the second time to this convent which had been miraculously preserved, and was replaced in the cell where the Venerable Mother Anne of St. Bartholomew had breathed her last sigh. It is in this pious oratory her body still rests, and where we are allowed to venerate it. May she soon be raised to the altar!

In conclusion, we declare that, in mind and heart, we submit to all the ordinances of the Holy Roman Church, whether as to the titles of Saint or Blessed, or to the narration of virtues and miraculous works which have not yet been sanctioned by the sovereign authority of the Vicar of Jesus Christ.

LIFE OF BLESSED MOTHER ANNE OF
SAINT BARTHOLOMEW. WRITTEN
BY HERSELF

FIRST BOOK

CHAPTER I

BIRTHPLACE AND PARENTAGE

Country and Parentage of the Blessed Mother Anne of St. Bartholomew.

It was a modest village of old Castile, known by the name of Almendral, that had the glory of giving to the world and the Church that fortunate virgin for whom God reserved the most enviable title of Inseparable Companion of St. Teresa. She was born on the 1st of October in the year 1550, the feast day of St. Remy. Almendral, whose name her birth was to immortalize, was only a few leagues from Avila, where the seraphic Teresa of Jesus was, several years later, to bring back to Carmel its former splendor. God thus placed at a short distance from each other the cradles of the two virgins who were to be united by such intimate ties.

Anne of St. Bartholomew's father was Ferdinand Garcia, and her mother, Maria Mancanas. Their praise is complete and their name handed down with honor to future ages, when it is said they were worthy of her to whom they gave the light of day. The intensity of their faith would not permit them to delay the happiness of regeneration to the child whom God had just given them. The very day of her birth they carried her to the Church; she received holy baptism, and the name of Anne was given her.

To cause God to reign was the motto of these Christian spouses. With a zeal full of faith they jealously sought His glory. Ferdinand caused all the feasts of our Lord to be celebrated with pomp; his spouse with no less zeal had all the feasts of the Most Blessed Virgin celebrated—that of the Immaculate Conception in particular. This was sufficient to delight the heart of God and draw down upon them and their family His continued blessings. Besides the graces with which God had inundated such faithful and fervent souls He was moreover pleased to bless their labors and make fertile their fields. Thus everything prospered in the home of Ferdinand Garcia and Maria Mancanas. No family in Almendral was held in such high esteem; it held the first rank there. Their abode was that of charity itself; the poor found there the most kindly welcome. So great was the tender compassion of Maria Mancanas that she could not hear a child weeping on the street without immediately inquiring into its trouble; and if it was an orphan she would adopt it and be to it as a mother.

God gave this holy couple seven children—three sons and four daughters. She whose Life you are about to read was the last. Wishing to raise them all in the fear of the Lord, they received into their home a virtuous ecclesiastic, to aid them in their pious design. God was therefore to reign in this blessed family. Every

3

Life of Blessed Anne of St. Bartholomew

day, without exception, the father, mother and all the children assisted at Holy Mass; every day prayers were said in common in the private oratory. There they recited the rosary of the Blessed Virgin. The priest, to whom Ferdinand Garcia had confided the care of his children, gave them every day a lesson in Christian doctrine; he taught them to fear and love God. The daughters never left the house except to go to church or to work in the fields. Thus her paternal home was like a monastery to the young virgin whom God called to live in the Order founded by St. Teresa. The example of her father and mother, of her brothers and sisters, could not but excite her to serve God. To crown her happiness, her first cousin, Francesca Garcia, born the same day and baptized the same date, like herself a miracle of innocence, and transplanted with her to Carmel, was her inseparable companion and confidential friend until the greatly desired moment when, bidding a final farewell to Almendral, they set out for Avila to be clothed there, in the monastery of St. Joseph, with the habit of Our Lady of Mount Carmel.

CHAPTER II

HORROR OF SIN

Her First Vision at About the Age of Three Years—Horror of Sin—Her Devotion to the Blessed Virgin, St. Joseph, the Saints and Angels.

Jesus, Mary, Joseph, and our holy Mother, Teresa of Jesus, in whose names I undertake this work, commanded me by holy obedience.

I was very small, not knowing yet how to speak, when one day they put me on my feet in a room where my sisters were working. My mother, passing by, said to them: "Be very careful that the little one does not fall, as she might kill herself." One of my sisters then said: "God would do her a great favor, if she died, for now she would go to heaven." "Do not say that," replied another of my sisters. "May she not die; for, if she lives, she may become a saint." "That is doubtful," replied the first. "Now there is no danger for her; while children who have reached the age of seven years, may sin." I heard all this, and when my sister uttered the word "sin" I raised my eyes to heaven, without knowing, as it seemed to me, what I was doing, and I thought that I saw the heavens open, and our Lord appeared to me in great majesty. As it was something new, I felt pierced to the heart with fear and reverence for Him who was present, for I recognized that it was God, and that it was He who would judge me. From this moment there was ever within me a great fear of sin, as my sisters called it, and of offending God.

Having reached the age of seven years, the thought came to me one day that I might, perhaps, have the misfortune to sin, and I wept. One of my sisters asked me why I wept. I answered, "Because I fear to commit sin, and I would rather die."

Because of this fear I began to have devotion towards several saints, but, before all, to the holy angels and to St. Joseph, whom, in my childlike simplicity, I took to be an angel. It was, however, the most holy Virgin who had my first homage. I had great confidence in her. I honored also the Eleven Thousand Virgins, St. John Baptist, and others among the blessed. Every day I begged them to keep me from sin, and I begged them particularly for the virtue of chastity. With such intercessors before God, I lived in great consolation and was very devoted to the good Jesus. I felt in my soul wonderful movements of His love, and in all that I did my only desire was that my Jesus should see me, that He should look at me and be contented with me. These were my habitual desires and thoughts when I was alone. I would look out of the windows into the fields to see if I could perceive Him, and this I did with great simplicity.

At this tender age, when I was with other little girls, and they played, I wished to play with them also. One day, being in prayer

5

Life of Blessed Anne of St. Bartholomew

and greatly consoled (they were no doubt the consolations of little children), I said to our Lord: "My Lord, give me permission to go play with my companions, and I will return immediately after." And it seemed to me that our Lord granted it to me with pleasure.

When I passed a day without addressing prayers to the Saints, to whom I had devotion, I was suddenly troubled with the fear of making them displeased with me; I made great haste to ask their pardon, and promised to be faithful in honoring them.

This is what passed in my soul until the tenth year of my life. At this age I lost my parents and their loss cast me into the deepest affliction.

CHAPTER III

NEW FAVORS

New Favors—Apparition of the Infant Jesus—Holy Friendship With Her Cousin—Their Attempt to Fly Into the Desert.

I remained in the homestead with my brothers and sisters, who were to me father and mother; they were truly very good. As soon as I was old enough they sent me to guard the flocks in the fields; it was only a short distance from our home. At first I experienced great pain, but soon our Lord consoled me, and the fields became for me a source of delight. The birds by their songs led my soul into recollection. Therefore, as soon as they began to sing, I entered into a state of recollection which lasted entire hours. And very often when I was in this state the Infant Jesus came and placed Himself in my arms. I would find Him in this position when I would come to myself. What my soul experienced during this recollection I do not know how to express. I found myself in a glorious heaven, where I would have liked to live always. I desired never to see anyone again, and to go to a distant desert. Once I said to the Infant Jesus: "My Lord, since you are keeping me company, do not let us go any more where there are other persons, but let us go alone to some mountains, for with your company nothing will be wanting to me." But He smiled and, without speaking, made me understand that was not what He wanted of me. I already loved solitude so much because of this company that it was death to me to meet others. Sometimes night surprised me without my having perceived it, when half a league from the house. My brothers, frightened at this delay, would come to seek me, and would scold me. I was not at all astonished at their reproaches, as they did not know the company I enjoyed, and as I never spoke a word of it to them they might have thought something else.

I lived in such high prayer without knowing what it was that ordinarily I was all inflamed with the love of Jesus. I commenced to think how I could manage to go to some place where no one would know I was a woman, and where I would be despised by everyone. For this end I thought of putting on man's clothes and flying. I saw that by doing this I would give cause for evil thoughts of me, but I feared nothing, and no obstacle presented itself to my mind that I was not ready to surmount. I did not consult with anyone about these things, except with a relative of my own age, who had received baptism at the same time with me. She was very good and had excellent aspirations. When we went to Mass, or could be together, our hearts, it seemed to me, were set on fire with the love of God. I said to her one day: "My sister, why should not we two go to some desert, dressed as men, and spend our lives doing penance, like Magdalen?" She was

7

Life of Blessed Anne of St. Bartholomew

more prudent than I, and replied: "My sister, it is no longer the time to do that; there are a thousand difficulties and a thousand dangers." Notwithstanding this reply, I did not fail to urge her often on this point, and ended by conquering her. I told her then that we would disguise ourselves as poor women slaves and strangers, and would go away in the night. Thus it was arranged; it was decided that on a certain night, while all were sleeping, we would carry out our design. The moment having arrived, we thought to meet with no obstacle; but our Lord did not will it. We both struggled all night, and it was impossible for us to go out; though it would appear easy to open the doors, we could not, however, succeed in doing it. In the morning we found ourselves together at the church, and each one put to the other this question: "Well, why did you not leave?" We could not help laughing on seeing how the Divine Master had spoiled our plan. I must add that we had agreed together to paint our faces, so as not to appear like women. We did this with so firm a determination, and such good will, that, had the Master been willing, nothing else, it seems to me, would have been wanting. The secret was kept perfectly by both of us. We were in some sort but one soul, only my companion was much better than I.

CHAPTER IV

TRIALS FROM HER FAMILY

Her Brothers Think of Establishing Her in the World—Her Plea to the Blessed Virgin to Have No Other Spouse But Her Son—Her Mortifications—Victory Won Over the Enemy of Our Salvation—Her Vocation to Carmel Revealed to Her by the Blessed Virgin.

My brothers, seeing that I was of the proper age, thought of establishing me in the world; but I had no thoughts of this kind. I called the Blessed Virgin, whom I had taken as my mother, and all my well-beloved Saints, and I increased my devotions and penances. I went to the church, I hid myself in a chapel of the Conception of Our Lady, and there, with bare feet and knees on the ground, I supplicated this Divine Mother to come to my aid.

At this time I found myself assailed by a thousand terrible temptations contrary to my will. It was for me a torment and an affliction. To this was joined the snares of the devil; but I took the discipline; I went down into a damp cave, and, prostrate on the earth, remained in prayer until the fury of the temptation had ceased. I slept on broken crockery, I clothed my body in some coarse linen in place of my tunic, which I gave to the poor, in order that it would not be noticed in the house that I did not wear it; and at other times I put on haircloth.

Once they ordered me to lie down with one of my sisters who was frightened. I had not yet recited my rosary, and, in order not to fall asleep, I took with me a large stone, which was very sharp, and after having put out the light I went to bed, slipping this stone in also; it was the pillow I made use of very frequently. This time I put it directly under my body, in order not to go to sleep. But it was not sufficient, for before finishing my rosary I slept. During my sleep I saw the Mother of God, surrounded with great splendor, carrying the Infant Jesus in her arms, enter the room. Seated with Him on a brilliant throne, she regarded me with kindness. The Divine Child commenced to pull me with the rosary, as if He wished to play, and drew me so forcibly that He awakened me. The Mother of God then said to me: "Have no anxiety and fear nothing; I will lead you, myself, to the place where you will be a religious, and where you will wear my habit." Having said these words, she disappeared. I remained supremely consoled, and with the most ardent desire to serve my God.

Another day, when my relatives were persecuting me, to force me to yield to their desires that I should be married, this thought came to my mind: If there was to be found a just man who was very prudent and very handsome—for it seemed to me I had never seen such a one as I imagined; on the contrary, they were all ugly, in my opinion—if, as I said, I should meet such an upright one, I would say to myself that I would not sin by accepting him as

Life of Blessed Anne of St. Bartholomew

a spouse, for I would have in him a support, and he would be the guardian of my virginity; but if he were not such, I would not have him for the whole world.

One day Jesus appeared to me, partly grown up, a little less in height than a young man. He was wonderfully beautiful, and this ennobling beauty shone forth from His whole Divine Person. From my most tender childhood, when He appeared to me in the fields, or elsewhere, He was always my height, so that it seemed as if He grew with me. In this last apparition He was as I have just described. He spoke these words to me: "I am He whom thou lovest and with whom thou must contract the union of espousals." He disappeared immediately, but my soul remained ravished and inflamed with love of Him. And from that time the outbursts of love that I experienced usually were so impetuous they deprived me of my natural strength. Day and night I had no other thought but of what I could do for the Well-Beloved. I wished to endure for Him labors, affronts, and to be considered as a fool.

Once one of my married sisters sent me a message to go to her house. "Is there anyone with her?" I asked the servant. "Yes," she replied; "a young man, her husband's brother." Now I knew my brother-in-law and sister wished to marry me to this young man and they made efforts to bring it about. I made a toilet according to my own fashion. I took some coarse clothes from the kitchen, put them on as carelessly as possible, and in this costume started for my sister's house. Scarcely had she seen me, as I crossed the threshold of the door, than she became unusually annoyed, and said to me: "Where are you going? Are you a fool? Go away from here." And I returned home full of joy.

CHAPTER V

CONSTANCY AND RECOLLECTION

Her Constancy and Her Recollection—Words That She Addressed to Our Lord—The Divine Master Shows Her, in a Vision, the Monastery of the Religious of St. Joseph at Avila.

I avoided speaking with men and of giving them occasion to speak to me. If my brothers' friends entered the house I went out, or I showed them a face which would impress them as if they had had a frightful apparition. I used this prudent reserve because, as I have said, I often felt within myself a strong determination to serve our Lord, and I realized besides the obligations I had towards my God: they were great and required of me great purity and fidelity. These were the two considerations that animated me to combat manfully against the world.

I was sometimes sent, together with my sisters and the servants of the house, a quarter of a league from the village to a place where we had wheat fields and flocks. All the way there I kept silence, and, as soon as we arrived, would seek a secluded spot under the trees, tell them not to disturb me, and then enter into prayer. The good Jesus would come near me and sit down, as I have already mentioned. I would say to Him: "Let us go away, my Lord, to some solitary place." In very truth He showed that He would do this with pleasure, but that it was not suitable; He made me understand this without speaking, but only by looking at me with a divine smile. For my part, I desired to go to the high mountains which were not far distant; and, this time, He made me understand it could not be. I, however, asked Him again to lead me to some solitary mountain, and after that request I slept for awhile. He showed me, then, the Monastery of Avila, which was the first our holy Mother had succeeded in founding; also the religious of this monastery wearing the habit. I asked them for something to drink, as I was thirsty. All this passed in my sleep. They gave me a drink, and I recognized afterwards, when I was in the monastery, the glass they had offered me with the water. This vision took away my desire to go to the desert, and I had no longer any other desire than to be a religious.

CHAPTER VI

JOURNEY TO AVILA

She Makes Known to Her Spiritual Guide Her Desire to Be a Carmelite at Avila—She Sees the Heavens Opened—Her Journey to Avila—The Religious Accept Her, But Delay Her Entrance—Return to Almendral—A Host of Demons Appear to Her on the Way.

At this time it pleased God to send as pastor of the church of this town a priest who was a Doctor of Divinity and a great servant of God. My companion and I made our confessions to him. When I made known to him that I wished to be a religious at Avila, he said to me: "They have just founded a new monastery; if you wish me to speak with the religious and ask a place for you, I will do so." It seemed as if heaven had opened to me, and I replied yes, that it would console me very much. He did so with paternal solicitude, though I had been confessing to him for so short a time. He made known my desires, and they replied to him in the monastery to send me to Avila, as they wished to see me before coming to any decision. After this reply, I made known to my brothers the desire I had to be a religious; I told them I had already communicated with the monastery, and the religious wished to see me. My brothers were much distressed; but, as they had a holy fear of God, they did not refuse me, and accompanied me to Avila. By a particular dispensation of God, the religious accepted me immediately, with pleasure. For my part, I experienced great content to find myself with them, and I recognized those I had seen in my dream. But this was only a simple interview, and it was arranged between us that they would let me, as well as my relatives, know when I should return. My brothers said to me: "Why do you wish to join these religious? They seem to us very austere." I answered them: "They seem to me like saints." And it was as if I had been with them all my life.

When we were returning my relatives seated themselves near a spring to rest; I went aside and, when alone, raised my eyes to God to thank Him for the favor He had granted me. But when the evil spirit saw me returning to the world, and as the secrets of God are unknown to these spirits of darkness, I saw a great troop of demons suddenly assemble before me and in the air; they danced with great demonstrations of joy, as if they already had me in their power; they looked like men very diminutive in form, having, as it were, only claws and heads, horrible to look upon, and so numerous that they cast a shadow like a flock of birds. If God did not permit them to succeed in what they thought of doing, He at least allowed them to make war on me, either through relatives and friends, or by interior and exterior diabolical temptations. If they had molested me before, they did so now with much greater fury. But God did not allow them to act according to their will, and if He doubled the temptations He doubled my spirit of recollection and my strength to resist them.

12

CHAPTER VII

PROTECTION OF GOD

Trials to Which She is Subjected by Her Brothers—Miraculous Strength Given Her by God—How Wild Bullocks Become Like Lambs at the Sound of Her Voice, and How They Defend Her—Her Cousin and Herself Find Themselves Exposed to a Great Danger—The Divine Master Protects and Delivers Them.

My brothers threatened me in order to try me. From threats they soon passed on to deeds. They made me share the tasks of the day laborers who worked in the fields. They gave me, besides, other duties which required the strength of a man. The servants of the house said that two of them together could not do what I did alone. I laughed at their talk, as the burden I was ordered to carry seemed to me only a straw. I was interiorly so intoxicated with divine love, and my mind was so actively employed, that I could not have borne it if the painful labors imposed upon me had not come to distract me. My brothers did not spare me; they gave me two carts to draw alone; they were not smaller than wagons; they were used to carry the sheaves of wheat from the field to the barn, where they were to be threshed. The harvesters made sheaves for me twice as large as those for the men, thinking that I could not lift them. I took them up, however, with great ease, and threw them without any effort into the carts. Seeing this, the men who were reaping stopped to gaze at me; they seemed seized with fear, and asked one another if this strength came from God or from the evil spirit.

The sheaves of wheat having been carried to the threshing-floor, I was told to thresh them. In order to do this I was obliged to harness two or three pairs of oxen; they were unruly and difficult to manage; but God gave me so much strength that when I called them they immediately bowed their heads and came of their own accord to receive the yoke, as if they had been lambs.

One day they sent me to find these oxen when they were in pasture. One was missing; he had remained among the briars between the rocks. While I was seeking him I saw a mad dog coming; I did not know it was mad; but soon it sprang at me and tried to bite me. I threw myself face downward on the ground, that I might not feel its breath; it jumped on me and tore my clothes, which were new and which I wore that day for the first time. The ox I could not find was hidden quite near. As soon as he saw I was thus badly treated by the dog, he came out of the brushwood, darted forward to my aid, and attacked the dog, which soon left me. The animal then approached me, as if he had been endowed with reason; he licked and caressed me with his mouth. He then started forward and made me a sign to lean on him. I did

Life of Blessed Anne of St. Bartholomew

so, and he conducted me in this way to the house, to the great astonishment of all who witnessed it.

Another time I went with my cousin to guard the flocks at the foot of the mountain. We were seated on a rock when we saw afar off a shepherd coming towards us. We were afraid and hid ourselves in a cave which was under this rock; as the grass was high there, we laid down in it. We were alone and defenseless; but God wished to protect us. The man came, he even stepped upon the rock where he had seen us, and, not being able to find us, he cried out: "Where can they have gone? May the devil take them!" We remained hidden until evening, and did not leave our hiding place until we thought he had gone. But, owing to fright, we were so bathed in perspiration, one would have thought we had come out of the river.

On my return to the house they reproached me most severely; they told me I was foolish, that I must renounce prayer and the idea of becoming a religious; that if I went to the convent at Avila I could not endure the austerity; that I would be obliged to return, and that I would dishonor the family; that it would be better to stop short and prevent this misfortune by no longer thinking of entering the monastery. To accomplish this design, sometimes my relatives treated me with severity and again with much affection. According to them, they acted in this way only for my good; if they opposed my wishes, it was only because I had not the strength to bear the kind of life I wished to embrace. They made use of their friends to turn me from my resolution, to counsel me as my relatives counseled me—in a word, to tell me that I was not in a good way and must take another.

CHAPTER VIII

APPARITIONS

On a beautiful moonlight evening one of my relatives asked my brother's permission to take me with her to see her linen, which was in a house not far from the hamlet. Scarcely had we arrived when we heard a great noise that frightened me exceedingly; there was dragging of chains and loud groans. My relative, seeing that I was disturbed, said to me: "It is nothing; it is only some animal passing on the road." But soon there appeared to us at a short distance a frightful apparition. It was someone twice the height of a man; notwithstanding his great size, he was very agile, and he advanced towards us. Seeing this, I fanted and fell to the ground, saying: "May the Most Holy Trinity assist me!" My companion quickly raised me up and endeavored to calm my fear. Seeing that I was somewhat restored, though very weak, she supported me with her arm, and took me back to the house. Now, during all the time of our walk, from the linen-house to my home, I saw at a little distance three persons clothed in white, constantly walking before us. I said to my relative, "Who are those persons?" "They must be," she said, "shepherds returning from guarding their flocks." But on reaching the house I recognized by a supernatural light that it was the Most Holy Trinity whom I had called to my aid. I still suffered from the fear and weakness of heart caused by the frightful vision of which I have just spoken. That night I could not remain alone in a room without being seized with fright. It was as if a wicked shadow pursued me. I spoke of it to my brothers; they had Masses offered for my relief, but the trial did not cease. It was then near the Feast of St. Bartholomew, and there was, five leagues distant from Almendral, a hermitage of that holy Apostle, for which they had great devotion in these parts. My relatives took me there to make a novena. When three leagues from our destination I asked permission to go on foot, in order that God might grant the favor of my cure. They consented. I then walked the three leagues. But on arriving at the hermitage, feeling extremely fatigued, I wished, before entering, to rest for a few minutes, when suddenly I was struck with paralysis. It was necessary to carry me into the sanctuary consecrated to the Apostle. Scarcely had I crossed the threshold than I felt delivered from my illness and completely cured. To crown my happiness I received the assurance that I would see the accomplishment of my desires.

CHAPTER IX

HER ENTRANCE INTO RELIGION

Her Entrance Into Religion Retarded by Her Relatives—Recourse to the Souls in Purgatory, and to the Blessed Virgin—Constancy in Her Vocation—Entrance Into the Monastery of St. Joseph at Avila on All Souls' Day.

On our return from the pilgrimage to St. Bartholomew we received letters from the Monastery of St. Joseph, whither they bade me come. But there was no sign that my relatives were willing to give their consent. I had a Mass said every day for a year for the souls in purgatory, that these souls by their influence, and the Blessed Virgin by her power, would change my relatives. They put off their consent from day to day, thinking that these delays would end by making me give up my intention.

During this interval, several religious, who were going to make a foundation in Talavera, passed through Almendral. My relatives begged them to accept hospitality with us. Seizing so good an occasion, they entreated the religious in the name of God to persuade me to go with them, saying that the monastery they were about to found was very near, and that they would be much better contented to have me with them. The religious did not fail to advise according to the wishes of my relatives. They shut themselves up all evening with me, pressing me with the greatest earnestness; they made me the most advantageous offers, and promised me all the favors imaginable. But the greater the efforts they made to persuade me the stronger and more determined I felt not to depart from what our Lord had shown me. It was undoubtedly that Divine Master who gave me the strength, for naturally I should certainly have desired the honors these servants of God promised me, and the advantage of being near my relatives. But that which might have been agreeable to others I held in horror. Finally God came to my help, and the thought of changing my resolution never entered my mind.

For their part, the religious of St. Joseph at Avila wrote pressing letters for me to come; my brothers replied that they would take me on the Feast of All Saints.

The eve of this feast my brothers were discontented, and said nothing to me. The hour for supper having come, and being at table with my three sisters and two of my brothers, I asked them if we were not going on our journey. At these words my oldest brother was seized with such a fit of anger that he rose from the table and drew his sword to kill me. One of my sisters rose and caught his hand, or, rather, I believe it was one of God's angels, for I saw the sword giving me the blow on the head. And God gave me, in so short a space of time, such perfect resignation to die for love of Him, that I hope to have as great at the hour of

16

Her Entrance Into Religion

death. I said in my heart to the Divine Master: "My Lord, I die very contentedly, for the sake of justice." The sister who held my brother's hand said to me: "Go away from here; leave our presence and cease troubling the house." I went to hide myself in a secret place, and left them greatly troubled; they were in such a state that all night they had no thought of looking for me. It seemed as if a multitude of evil spirits were going through the whole house. In the morning I slipped out without any one seeing me and went to Church. My confessor on seeing me said: "How is this that you have not started yet for the convent?" I told him what had happened, and that I only came to go to confession. For my part I was not at all angry with them. I saw plainly they were not to blame; it was the devil who was doing it all. My confessor ordered me to communicate. I told him that I scrupled to receive Holy Communion without having begged their pardon. He replied that there was no cause for it, but finally let me go. I went on my knees and asked their pardon. They replied in a rough tone: "Go out of here; how can you come again after all the pain you have caused us?" I went out without any reply and communicated. After Communion I became somewhat recollected, and divided between pain and content I gave thanks to God for all. While I was thus recollected, thanking my God for all the favors He had showered on me, my brother entered the church, the very one who had wished to kill me. In the excess of the grief my departure caused him, his face was as that of one dead. He told me that everything was ready, and that I could return to the house. I was distressed to see my brother so disturbed, for he had an angelic character, and was, of all my brothers, the one I loved the most. He wished to accompany me, as well as that one of my sisters who had averted the blow; several other persons also joined us. During all the way they did nothing but weep, and could scarcely address a word to me. As for me, I trembled interiorly with joy; on the other hand, however, I was so tormented with wicked temptations it seemed as if all hell was leagued to war against me. I took care not to say the least word about this to those who accompanied me; for if I had been ever so little communicative, they would have had just cause to tell me that I was a fool to enter the monastery in such a condition.

The Holy Souls in Purgatory aided me to arrive at St. Joseph of Avila on their feast day, and the morning of this same day I saw the doors of the monastery opened to me. I had scarcely crossed the threshold than all this interior tempest was in a moment calmed; it was as if a veil had been lifted from above my head. I felt as if in heaven, so happy was I; it seemed to me that from my earliest childhood until this, I had lived this kind of a life and had dwelt among these saints.

SECOND BOOK

CHAPTER I

OBJECT OF VOCATION TO CARMEL

Of the End Mother Teresa of Jesus Proposed to Herself in Founding Her
Monasteries, How High and Perfect this Object Was, and What New
Value It Gave to the Order of Mount Carmel.

COMMENTARY

Before considering Anne of St. Bartholomew during the exercises of the novitiate, it is necessary to have a correct idea of
the Order to which God had called her. For this purpose we will
place before the eyes of our readers the end Saint Teresa proposed
to herself in founding her Order and the kind of rule observed
in it. It is the Saint herself, and Ribera, the most reliable of
her historians, to whom we shall listen. Their enlightened words
reveal to every reader the grandeur of Saint Teresa's mission
in the Church of God, and they give full knowledge of the Order
of Carmel.

We quote from Ribera: "Before going further with this narrative, it would be well, it seems to me, to satisfy the desire of
those who wish to know the end proposed by Mother Teresa of
Jesus in founding this monastery, and the rule, habit and manner
of life she established. That which we are about to say of the
House of St. Joseph at Avila applies equally to all the monasteries of which we shall speak later on.

"The intention of the Saint was only, in the beginning, to
found a monastery where she and those who wished to follow
her, could, by means of a stricter enclosure and a more austere
life, keep what they promised our Lord, conformably to the vocation of their Order; as for founding a new Order, the Holy Mother
never thought of that; she only hoped to restore in its primitive
perfection the ancient Order of Our Lady of Mount Carmel, in
which she had made her profession.

"Later, considering the great needs of the Church, and, in
her great charity, wishing, as far as lay in her power, to come to
the aid of those who were fighting for her, she went farther in
her design — she added to the penance and poverty she had at
first wished to introduce, and she made her foundation after another manner. But, as I desire that all this should be known from
her own words rather than from mine, I will relate here what she
herself says in the first chapter of her 'Way of Perfection.' I will
not cite from the edition of Evora or of Salamanca, but from the
very autograph of the Saint, which I have in my hands; it will
be the same with all the other quotations I will make in this work.
The Saint expresses herself thus: 'In the beginning, when making the foundation of this monastery of St. Joseph at Avila, it
was not my intention that they should lead so austere a life there,

nor that it should be without a revenue. On the contrary I would have liked to have sufficient resources so that nothing should be wanting. Such a desire makes known my weakness and my want of virtue; however, in inclining towards this view I had upright intentions, and sought to follow them rather than to flatter my nature. But having learned at this time of the blows dealt the Catholic faith in France, the ravages the unfortunate Lutherans had made there and the rapid inroads this disastrous sect was daily making, my soul was consumed with grief. From this time, as if I could do or was anything, I wept at our Lord's feet and begged Him to provide a remedy for so great an evil. I would willingly have given a thousand lives to save one of these souls whom I beheld perishing in such great numbers in that kingdom. But, alas! being a woman and still very weak in virtue, I saw the impossibility of serving in any way the cause of my Divine Master. However, I was continually pursued by a desire which still consumes me: seeing that my Divine Master had so many enemies and so few friends, I wished at least that these last should be invulnerable. Therefore, I resolved to do the little that depended on me, that is to say, to follow the evangelical counsels with all the perfection of which I was capable, and to lead the religious gathered at St. Joseph to embrace the same manner of life. I placed my confidence in the goodness of God, which never fails to assist those who generously renounce all for love of Him. My companions being such as I wished them to be, I hoped that my faults would be concealed by their virtues, and that thus I could, in some way, give pleasure to God. Finally, it seemed to me, by being entirely occupied in prayer for the defenders of the Church, for the preachers and wise men who fought for her, we would, as far as in our power, come to the aid of this Adorable Master so maliciously persecuted. Seeing the zeal with which these traitors, who had been loaded by Him with favors, made war against Him, one would think they wished to crucify Him anew and leave Him no place on earth where He might lay His head.' The Saint then adds: 'O my Sisters in Jesus Christ, unite with me in begging with most ardent supplications this favor of the Divine Master: this is your vocation; this is your business; towards this should all your aspirations tend; it is for this object your tears should flow; indeed, it is this you should never cease asking of God.' "

"These words of the Saint show clearly the end she proposed in the reform of her Order and in the foundation of her monasteries, also the vocation of the religious who dwell in them. Thus, although her first design was of great perfection, she nevertheless transformed it in such a way, she raised it so high by this new idea and end she gave it, that one can scarcely find in any Order of women perfection so great, nor a more exalted vocation. For, according to the teaching of St. Thomas and of truth, the superiority of one religious Order over another, as regards perfection, does not consist in the penances practised there, but in the privi-

Life of Blessed Anne of St. Bartholomew

lege of having a higher end, with means proportioned to the attainment of this end. Therefore, he concludes, the religious Orders highest in perfection are those which have for their end teaching and preaching, and that after them follow immediately the contemplative Orders; for, as it is better to enlighten others than only to shine oneself, so it is better to communicate to others what one has learned in contemplation than merely to contemplate. Now, as religious Orders of women are not established to preach, the highest Order among them would be the one which would have for end to aid by its prayers and penances those who fulfill this ministry; that is to say, those who defend the Church; for that mode of life is more perfect which approaches nearest to that which possesses the height of perfection; and no religious Order of women can have a higher end than that of unceasingly praying, fasting, leading a life of austerity, for the preservation and defense of the Catholic Church, and the salvation of souls, doing all in their power that the faithful may live according to their state, and that infidels may obtain knowledge of their Creator. To the truth of this, St. Gregory testifies in his 12th Homily on Ezechiel, where he says, 'that there is no sacrifice more agreeable to God than zeal for souls.' Another truth which proceeds from the words of the Saint, and which her religious should always have present to the mind and graven in their souls, is this: that, no matter what penances and what prayers they offer; how great their zeal in the choir and their fidelity to perform all that good and perfect religious should do, they do not fulfill the end of their vocation, nor what God demands of them, if they are not exceedingly careful to offer the prayers, fasts and penances of which we have spoken, for this exalted end, namely, of coming to the aid of those who are on the battlefield, struggling, combating for the glory of our Lord God; and finally for all those who in different parts of the world labor in an especial manner for the salvation of souls. From this it follows that what would suffice for other religious would not be sufficient for them; that what would be perfection for others would not be perfection for them; as they would be wanting in the principal thing in their vocation and their Order. As for me, I rejoice that this is written here, because every time it is read I will be proclaiming aloud, after my death, what I proclaim now during my life. And let the religious of this Order who will read this believe that the most holy Virgin Mary, who is the Mother of these monasteries; the blessed St. Joseph, who is their Father, and the holy Mother Teresa of Jesus, who is their Foundress, wish and desire that this doctrine should be preached in these monasteries. If one reads the works of the Saint attentively, they will see that what I have said, and will say again, to her religious, is what she, herself, has most expressly recommended in her writings. Thus, regarding the subject of which we are now treating, the holy Mother, after having said in the 13th chapter of the 'Way of Perfection' many excellent things, concludes with these words:

Object of Vocation to Carmel

" 'And when you do not refer your prayers, your desires, your disciplines, your fasts, to the end which I have pointed out to you, think and believe that you are not doing what God requires of you, and that you do not fufill the end for which He has assembled you here. May this Adorable Master, I beg of Him in the name of all that He is, never permit this to be effaced from your memory.' "

(Ribera, Life of St. Teresa, Book II, Chapter I.)

CHAPTER II

NOVITIATE OF BLESSED MOTHER

Anne of St. Bartholomew in the Novitiate—Trials—How Our Lord Engraved in Her Soul the Distinctive Characteristic of a Carmelite—Zeal for the Salvation of Souls—He Shows Her France; and the Sight of the Souls Going to Perdition in That Kingdom Redoubles the Ardor of Her Zeal—State of Her Soul During the First Fifteen Years of Her Religious Life.

Scarcely had I passed a few days in the Monastery of St. Joseph than it pleased our Lord to hide Himself from me and leave me in darkness. My desolation was great. I said to this Adorable Master: "How is this? Why have you abandoned me? If I did not know you, I would think you had deceived me, and if I had known you would go away I would not have come to the monastery."

This abandonment lasted during the entire year of novitiate. At the end of the year I entered one day the hermitage of Christ at the Pillar to pray. Scarcely had I knelt down than I became supernaturally recollected, and our Lord appeared to me fastened to the cross. The first words He addressed to me were in reply to a desire I had to know whether the thirst He experienced on the cross was a natural thirst. He said to me: "My thirst was only a thirst for souls. From henceforth you must apply yourself to the consideration of this truth, and you must walk in a different path from that you have followed until now." As if He had said to me, "Child, no longer seek Me." He then caused me to see all virtues in their perfection; they were exquisitely beautiful. I was the more impressed when I realized how far I was from their beauty and perfection. After having favored me with this light, the Divine Master disappeared, leaving my heart deeply wounded with His love, as well as by seeing Him on the cross so deeply wounded with the love of souls. This grace remained so indelibly impressed in my soul that it was with me day and night; my heart was with my Adorable Master, and my Adorable Master was in my heart; this was my usual state. Wherever I might be I experienced a zeal beyond expression for the salvation of souls and for the acquisition of those virtues that the Divine Master had shown me in the vision I have just related. He told me that it was by the way of the cross I would acquire them.

Another day I went to pray in the hermitage of St. Francis. Before entering I noticed a delightful perfume of flowers, which led me into profound recollection. I then beheld the Divine Master enter. His exterior was the same as when He was in this world. He was ravishingly beautiful, but He seemed exceedingly grieved. He approached me and put His right hand on my left shoulder. I felt a weight that I am unable to describe. This Adorable Master

22

communicated to my heart the pain that overwhelmed Him, and He said to me: "Behold the souls who are being lost in spite of My love. Aid Me to save them." And at the same time He showed me France, as if I were there, and the thousands of souls who are being lost because of heresies. This vision lasted scarcely a moment; if it had lasted longer I feel that I should have fallen. To tell the nature of the pain I experienced is something beyond my power. This vision and favor filled me with so great love for God and for souls I could scarcely live, so great was my thirst for their salvation. I had no desire to eat or sleep; thirst for the salvation of souls pursued me everywhere. There is no kind of penance I would not have wished to perform during these impetuous outbursts and states of fervor, and they lasted at least fifteen years; they had even commenced while I was still living with my family. If, during all this time, they had given me permission, I would have been foolish in performing penances, so insatiable was I for them. I did, however, all that depended on me to obtain permission, and when refused leave to use the discipline I asked that of pinching my arms. I did it so fiercely that they were all black from the wounds. I carried absinthe to the refectory, finely powdered, so that it would not be noticed, and I mixed it with my food.

My confessor, who knew the state of my soul, tried me in a thousand ways, in order to see if the Spirit of God was working in me.

One day I was greatly grieved concerning the state of several men who were being led to the gallows and who passed in front of our monastery. I could not keep back these words: "If I thought one of these men was not prepared to die, I would wish to be put in his place." The confessor said: "Your charity is not capable of that." I replied that it was, and that he should try me. My confessor then said: "Go to the fire and hold your finger in the flame for the space of a Credo; then come and tell me how you felt." Obedience made me brave; I did what the confessor commanded me and returned to give him an account. I do not know how it happened, but while I recited a Credo I held my finger in the fire, and I felt nothing—it caused me no pain. If I had done it of my own accord, I would have been frightened and thought the devil had purposed to deceive me; but as I did it through obedience I had no other thought than that God had commanded it. I returned, as I have said, to give an account to my confessor, and he said to me: "Go away from here. You are only a little fool. There is no common sense in all that."

After the fifteen years of which I have spoken, though my prayer was not always the same, and my soul was occupied sometimes with one object and sometimes with another, I was always aided by God to perform all the mortifications permitted me in the refectory and elsewhere. Often I rolled my naked body on thorns and nettles; but this must not be considered anything extraordinary, when the spirit is master of the flesh. I did many

Life of Blessed Anne of St. Bartholomew

things in order to pass for one who had lost her senses, as if I was very prudent!—certainly I had no need of artifices to appear devoid of sense—I was only too much so.*

FORMULA OF THE PROFESSION OF ANNE OF ST. BARTHOLOMEW

Literal extract from the Profession Book of the Convent of St. Joseph of Avila:

"On the 15th of August in the year 1572, his illustrious Lordship, Don Alavara de Mendoza, being Bishop of Avila, Sister Anne of Saint Bartholomew, known in the world as Anne Garcia Mancanas, made her profession in this house of Saint Joseph at Avila. She was a daughter of Ferdinand Garcia and Maria Mancanas, who lived in the village of Almendral. She gave as dowry 20,000 *maravedis;* she was twenty-one years of age when professed. Her profession was made in the following terms:

"I, Anne of St. Bartholomew, daughter of Ferdinand Garcia and Marie Mancanas, inhabitants of Almendral, make my profession, and promise obedience to Almighty God, the Virgin Mary, His glorious Mother, in whose name was founded the Order of Our Lady of Mt. Carmel, and to you, Most Reverend Sir, Ferdinand de Tricuela, Archdeacon of Arcoalo, Vicar General of the diocese of Avila, in the place of his Most Illustrious and Most Reverend Lordship, Don Alvaro de Mendoza, Bishop of Avila, and to the Bishops who will succeed him, and to you, Mother Mary of St. Jerome, Prioress of St. Joseph, and to the Prioresses who will succeed you in the said monastery, to live in poverty and chastity until death, according to the rule of Our Lady of Mount Carmel.

"Made this 15th day of August, 1572, and because it is the truth I sign it with my name or a cross."

(Then follows the signatures of the Prioress and two other religious. Anne of St. Bartholomew was professed as a lay-Sister.)

---

* We insert here something referring to this First Chapter. It is the formula of the profession of Anne of St. Bartholomew, as the Carmelites of St. Joseph of Avila wrote it in their Profession Book.

CHAPTER III

DEVOTION TO THE PASSION

Her Devotion to the Passion of Our Lord—Her Zeal in Imitating the Divine Master in His Sufferings—Her Tender Charity Towards the Poor—Vision of Purgatory—Prophetic Words of St. Teresa.

My soul was inflamed with love whenever I thought of the Passion of our Lord Jesus Christ; from my most tender years I had this devotion. Whilst still very small, when I entered the church and saw represented there the Passion of the Divine Savior, I would weep. I would have liked to be ill-used for love of Him. On leaving my home I would uncover my feet and walk on the stones and rough parts of the road, in order to be cut. What I could give away of my clothing, unnoticed, I would give, keeping the outer garments that could be seen, and giving the others to the poor. I put aside for them as much as possible; I hid for them what was given me for my meals. One day, one of my sisters said to me: "Have you eaten what was given you?" I replied, "Yes." My intention was to say, if the body had not eaten it, the soul had. I spoke of this once to my confessor, saying that I had deceived my sisters by telling them, with this intention, that I had eaten. I asked him if it was not a lie, for I would not willingly tell one for the whole world; and when I spoke in this way I believed I was telling the truth. He replied: "Who taught you that? Certainly there was no lie, since your intention was to give the repast to your soul." This is what I did to honor the Passion of Jesus Christ.

What I am about to say, and part of what has been said, is far from my subject, but I write it here for fear of forgetting it, as has been commanded me to do.

I will tell you what happened me one Good Friday when I was still very little. A great preacher visited our church. My sisters and I went to the sermon. I went with the ardent desire that the preacher would tell us wonderful things of the love with which Jesus Christ suffered. But the holy man said scarcely anything to my taste. I felt deeply pained during the whole sermon. It grieved me to hear him speak so coldly. I commenced to weep. My sisters said to me, "Little one, why do you weep?" I replied, "I weep because the Father did not preach well." They said, "What do you know about it?" "I assure you," I told them, "that if I could preach I would speak better on that subject, if I can judge by what I feel in my heart."

Once, when sleeping in our holy Mother's cell at Avila, I beheld myself in presence of our Lord Jesus Christ, who, as a Judge, was about to pass judgment upon me. I found myself, then, in purgatory. It was a vast expanse of water, one would say, the widest part of a great river; but in place of water it was all fire, and a fire which was suffocating in its intensity. I thought myself buried in the fire half way up my body. There were a great number of souls who were completely immersed in it; others not entirely. Being in the condition I have described, I saw my guardian angel coming toward me; he was very beautiful and wonderfully brilliant; he said to me: "Do you feel the fire very much?" "Yes," I said, "but with the hope of seeing our Lord soon, I do not suffer much pain." Wicked angels, armed with hooks, went along the border of the river, threatening to seize me, but they did me no harm. Soon the good angel, of whom I have spoken, came, and the vision disappeared. I awoke and I was as wet as if I had been thrown into the water, but I was quite glad to find that I was still living, for I thought the time of exile was over. This vision took place a few days after my entrance in the monastery of St. Joseph of Avila. When the Saint and the Sisters saw me they asked what had happened, for I had the appearance of one risen from the grave. I told the Saint what I had seen in sleep; she said to me laughingly: "Do not worry, my child; you will never go to purgatory." I considered these words as spoken through kindness, and never thought the Saint meant them otherwise; I thought, on the contrary, that I would have a long purgatory, and that God would do me a great favor to send me there rather than to a more frightful abyss, considering the way I have lived.

CHAPTER IV

LOVE OF GOD

How She Was Unceasingly Consumed With the Fire of Love of God and
Zeal for Souls, Without Being Able to Distract Herself—Her Con-
fessor Told Her It Was an Illusion, But St. Teresa Reassured Her—
How Our Lord Rewarded Her Obedience—Visit of the Divine Master,
When He Seemed to Take Away Her Heart—Vision in Which the
Eternity of God Was Made Manifest to Her.

I come back to that interior disposition which I commenced to
speak of; to those habitual outbursts of the love of God and those
transports of zeal excited by the sight of the souls our Lord had
shown me. All I could do was, in my opinion, little, in comparison
with my desires.

The confessor, noticing that this zeal and love for souls, which
never left me, lasted so long a time, said to me one day: "My
child, pay attention to me. This is a charity which comes from
the devil, and will end by deceiving you." I went to our holy
Mother and begged her to tell me if this was so, and gave an
account of all that had passed in me. She told me not to be
troubled, that this did not come from the demon; that she, herself,
had passed through this kind of prayer, and that she had met confessors who did not understand her. With this reply I was consoled, and I believed what the Saint told me—God, Himself, had
spoken through her mouth. It was not in my power to restrain
the love of God and zeal for souls that burned in my heart without ever leaving me. As I did not sleep, our Saint said one day
to me: "My daughter, as soon as the bell gives the signal for
retiring, leave your prayer and go to sleep." I wished to obey and
to do exactly what had been commanded me. Therefore, I said to
our Lord, when I was about to take repose: "My Lord, I have
not permission to remain with you; you must let me go to sleep."
Wonderful to relate—showing how our Lord wishes us to obey
—the Adorable Master allowed me to sleep as long as the others;
and on awaking I immediately found Him in my soul; it seemed
that He was there to guard and protect my sleep. My body was
filled with astonishing agility, it seemed no longer a human body;
so much so, that I feared some deceit, for, having so many duties
to fulfill, I rose up and walked about, feeling as light as a feather;
and in whatever place I might be, provided I was allowed a little
rest, I was filled with the love of God of which I have just spoken.

One day I was seated, occupied with my work, near the Turn—
for, in order to distract me, they gave me several offices. My soul
commenced to be more than usually inflamed with love of this
Divine Spouse; and whilst I was in this state the Divine Master
drew near to me, appearing exteriorly as when in this world. From
His manner of approaching me He seemed to have some particular

Life of Blessed Anne of St. Bartholomew

favor in reserve for me. Scarcely had He reached me, when He placed His hand on my heart, and it seemed to me He had taken it out. I experienced such intense pain that, spontaneously, without being aware of it, I uttered this compaint: "Why, my good Master, do you thus take away my heart?" He left it to me, however, but in such a way that it seemed to beg to leave my body, and was a prey to excessive pain. These visits made it impossible for me to distract myself.

Another day I was praying in a hermitage; I was raised to a supernatural state, and during this ecstasy I was shown the eternity of the Most Holy Trinity; and though this was truly shown me I do not know how to explain it; it lasted only a moment, the time of opening and closing the eyes; it is something beyond my comprehension. While I was in this state of recollection the bell called us to the refectory for collation. Without realizing it, and like one asleep, I rose up at the sound of the bell and went to the refectory; and it was not until after I was seated at the table, when some water fell on my hands, that I came to myself; it seemed as if I was awaking from a dream.

CHAPTER V

DUTIES APPOINTED HER

Extreme Feebleness to Which She is Reduced by Transports of the Love of God During One Year—The Divine Master Makes Known to Her That She is to Be Companion to St. Teresa, and That Both Could Satisfy Their Thirst for Suffering in Their Journeys Making Foundations—After a Year's Absence, St. Teresa Returns From Seville to Avila—She Cures the One Whom Our Lord Destines for Her Companion and Gives Her Care of the Sick—The Divine Master Assists Her in a Miraculous Manner.

Owing to the transports of love of God which I experienced, my nature and strength became so weak that it seemed I was about to give way. Physicians were called, but they did not understand my sickness. Some said that I was consumptive. They gave me several remedies, which only succeeded in ruining my constitution. I became so weak I was no longer able to raise my feet from the ground.

At this time our holy Mother left for Seville. She could not take me with her. As I had so great a desire for suffering, I said to the Divine Master: "Lord, I have asked Thee for sufferings, but now, as I realize those that I have add a burden to the community, I desire Thee to give me such as I can bear alone, so that I can serve my Sisters without increasing their labor. I wish these sufferings for myself." The Divine Master answered: "I will do what you ask of Me: you will have something to suffer together with my friend Teresa. You will both find in traveling the sufferings so ardently desired."

I continued, however, in the same condition until the return of our holy Mother from Seville. She had been absent one year. The Saint found me in a most miserable state; it seemed as if all my bones were dislocated. However, on the very evening of her return she said to me: "My daughter, come to my cell, even though you are ill just now." And, truly, to all appearance I was entirely incapable of serving her.

There were at that time five in the house ill with fever; one of them, Isabelle Baptist, was in great danger; besides the fever she had so great disgust for food she could take nothing. The day after her arrival, in the morning, the Saint said to me: "My daughter, though you are ill, I wish you to take charge of the sick, as there is no one else to attend to them." I said not a word, fearing to act contrary to obedience; but I thought to myself: "How can I fill this office, since I can scarcely lift my feet from the ground?" As well as I could I dragged myself to the kitchen to prepare something for the one who was most sick. To reach her cell I was obliged to go up a staircase of twelve steps. I stopped at the foot of the staircase and said to the Divine Master: "Lord, come to my aid; I cannot go up one single step." The

Life of Blessed Anne of St. Bartholomew

Adorable Master appeared then at the top of the staircase; He was ravishingly beautiful, as in the other apparitions, and under the same form as when He conversed with men. He said to me, "Ascend!" At this word I found myself at His feet, without having experienced the least suffering. He went with me to the cell of the sick one, He leaned over the head of the bed, like an infirmarian who wished to soothe the sick, and said to me: "Place here what you carry, and go give to the others what they need; I will Myself serve this one." I went, but I was cured; I felt as strong as if I had never had the least sickness; I hurried as fast as possible, earnestly hoping to find my dear Master on my return. But, notwithstanding all the haste I could make, when I returned I could not find Him. The sick one was radiant with joy; she said to me: "My Sister, what kind of dishes have you brought me? In all my life I have never eaten anything more to my taste." I did not tell her then of the vision I had had, notwithstanding the great friendship which existed between us. I asked her if, during my absence, some Sister had not been with her. She replied in the negative. At this reply I kept silence. She told me, however, that never before had she felt greater resignation or consolation in her soul, and that it seemed to her that she had no longer any trouble. Soon all my sick were cured, and the holy Mother said to me: "I make you Prioress of the sick; therefore, do not ask me any permission for what you consider necessary for them."

CHAPTER VI

APPOINTED TO CARE FOR THE SICK

Return of Fervor—Power of Obedience—Anne Charged With the Care of
the Sick and the Labor of the House—Assistance of Our Lord—
Heavenly Joy She Experiences in Taking Care of the Holy Mother
—A Sister Miraculously Cured—Words of the Divine Master, Which
Confirm Anne of St. Bartholomew in Her Great Desire to Serve All
the Sisters—Heroic Charity Which She Practises During Forty Days.

My fervor of the past returned. I had great need of exterior
occupations to resist it. I was like a man with a fine appetite who
has before him a great number of dishes which he devours with
his eyes, but who realizes if he indulges his appetite he will be
lost; he uses moderation, therefore, but the more he controls himself the greater his hunger becomes. I practised charity, seizing
every occasion that presented itself: I did this through the favor
of our Lord who had given me health and furnished me with occasions of practising this virtue towards my Sisters. I did not merit
it, but the Divine Master in His love enabled me to merit it.

The religious were greatly astonished when the holy Mother
ordered me to care for the sick, being at the time so ill myself, but
God permitted it so, that they might see the efficacy of the com-
mands of Superiors, and the wisdom which guided our holy Mother
in all that she commanded. In obeying her order I was cured.
All the Sisters were astonished beyond measure, and I more than
the others, knowing how unworthy I was of so great a favor.

While I was infirmarian I was obliged to take care of a religious
who was very ill. One day, seeing that she was resting, I left her
and went to hide for a little while in a cave to pray. While my
soul was recollected I heard a living voice saying to me: "Come,
rise up!" I replied, "My Lord, what is your command?"—for I
recognized His sweet voice; but He did not reply. I went out to
see what was wanted of me and learned that they were searching
for me all over the house, as the sick Sister had asked for me. As
soon as I reached her I saw that she had had a weak spell, and that
my attentions were indeed necessary.

Besides caring for the sick I had all the work of the house to
do, as the Saint had ordered. I also waited on the holy Mother
herself, thus enjoying her loving company, serving her with indescribable joy and an agility of body altogether supernatural, just
as one might expect of the Divine Master who worked all this
in me.

Another religious became very ill with a carbuncle on her eye.
This trouble is very dangerous in our country. The physicians
soon gave her up. The surgeon, however, continued his remedies.
One day, being obliged to leave the city to visit another patient,
he warned me very particularly not to allow anyone to touch the

31

Life of Blessed Anne of St. Bartholomew

wound until his return, adding that he would be back very soon. I gave this sick Sister all the care necessary, and I did so with such promptness and such agility, it seemed to me, I no longer felt the weight of my body. This Sister was a great servant of God. She was called Petronilla Baptist. At night I slept near her, and in my sleep I saw two religious of our Order enter. They seemed to me to be Elias and Eliseus. They drew near the sick one, they took away the bandage from the wound on her eyes and bathed them. The smaller one, who was Eliseus, came and went with what was necessary, with astonishing promptness. When they had finished their ministrations to the sick one, they said to me, "This is how you should take care of the sick, and not with the negligence you show." I understood by these words that our works appear very differently in the eyes of God than in the eyes of men. I thought I acquitted myself of my office very well, but I saw after this lesson that the best in me was very imperfect before God.

It was not because I was good that our Lord granted me these favors, but that His goodness might be made manifest. Although I was so unworthy of grace, this Adorable Master sought me out even when I was least occupied with the thought of Him, in order that I might not be lost, and that His kindness might cause admiration. I performed these labors with great consolation, when obedience ordained them. I had no merit in this; without thinking of the wickedness which must be in me and the numerous faults which escaped my attention, I found consolation in these labors, and it seemed to me I did all for the love of God. As my Adorable Master saw this, and because He loved me, He took care to send me certain trials, that I might see my self-love, and in order to temper my ardor.

At this time, when I had charge of these duties, and when I earnestly desired that obedience would allow me a little time to be alone with our Lord, I entered one day into a state of supernatural recollection after Communion; the Divine Master then said to me: "Arise! My will is that you should conform to the wishes of all the Sisters and in all that they command you." It was a great consolation for me to know that that was the will of our Lord. I was satisfied with these words, because they authorized me to go forward with greater liberty, for, naturally, I was much inclined to give pleasure, and I feared sometimes it might be a species of self-love; the Divine Master by these words relieved me of this doubt.

Another time I was seated near the door, as I was portress. I was feeling somewhat hurt, as it seemed to me the older Sisters were not satisfied that the Prioress had placed me at the Turn, because I was still young, and I thought that they were right under the present circumstances. In this mood I saw in spirit our Lord showing me a withered rosebush in the courtyard, all covered with red and white roses; as it was dried up and it was not the season of roses, the Divine Master said to me: "These roses cannot be gathered without encountering the thorns." He wished to make me understand, by that, that it is by sufferings and contradictions that virtue is acquired.

I will say here, for the glory of our Lord, that He always gave me consolation when I did good to my neighbor, when the occasion presented itself, and when I aided them in their need. I inconvenienced myself, it is true, on these occasions, but I found instead of an inconvenience it was a real consolation. It is to the good Master I owe it, and it has remained so with me until this day. May His holy Name be blessed!

By a secret of His love, the Divine Master wished to purify in the crucible of suffering one of His dearest spouses at St. Joseph of Avila; this religious was Anne of St. Peter. He sent her suddenly a terrible leprosy which covered her body. The angelic patient recognized this as a gift from the hand of her Well-Beloved and knew how to correspond with the designs of His love. The physicians advised that she should be sent away from the convent, fearing her sickness might be contracted, at least by those who must wait on her. God insired me with a great desire to take care of her. I spoke of it to a Sister who suddenly wished to aid me in order to prevent the sick one from leaving the convent. We went to find the Prioress, and begged her on our knees to permit us to take care of her, assuring her that we were ready to serve her in every way. Touched by our resolution, the Prioress consented with pleasure. The physicians ordered the most violent disinfectants. The convent was poor and could not provide the quantity of linens that would have been necessary. Therefore I was obliged to wash during the night the linens which had been used during the day, in order to give her always what was proper. Her body was one wound and her flesh began to putrefy; it exhaled an odor that we could never have been able to endure if God had not strengthened us, and this odor clung to everything that touched her body. I waited on her, therefore, during the day, and during the night I washed the linens infected with this intolerable odor of which I have just spoken. I did this for forty days in succession. Besides this I was obliged to serve at the Turn, as we were few in number. I did all this with an agility and ease that astonished me; God caused me to consider it as a recreation. The odor of the sick one was such that the others could not even pass near her cell. As for her, as I have said, she was an angel in virtue, and God loved her. He must, undoubtedly, have found great pleasure in seeing my companion and myself taking no account of our repugnances, and lavishing our care upon her. I felt neither fatigue nor the loss of sleep, nor want of nourishment; it was the same with my companion; it was evident that God was with us.

One day, touched by the excessive sufferings of the sick one, I begged the Divine Master to be pleased to relieve her. He replied that she had not yet gained sufficient merit, and that it was not time to free her from suffering. But at the end of forty days

Life of Blessed Anne of St. Bartholomew

her sufferings were exchanged for joy. I saw her, and our holy Mother, who was then at the Monastery of the Incarnation, also saw her, at the side of the Divine Master, who showed her much love and showered favors upon her. In order to increase her merits and sanctity God caused her to carry new crosses, interior as well as exterior. As Prioress, she governed in a saintly manner the Monastery of Avila. And later, when she had finally placed the last jewel in her crown of merit, I saw her ascend to heaven, all resplendent with glory.

CHAPTER VII

AFFLICTIONS

St. Teresa Breaks Her Arm—Affliction and Solicitude of Anne of St. Bartholomew—Apparition of Our Lord to His Servant Under the Form of the *Ecco Homo*—Another Apparition of the Divine Master, on Wednesday in Holy Week.

At this time our holy Mother broke her arm. She was on her way one evening to the Choir for Compline. It was already growing dark and she had a staircase to descend before entering the choir. The evil spirit threw her from the top of the staircase to the bottom. By the fall her arm was broken in the middle. The suffering she endured was great; all the Sisters sympathized deeply with her, and I more than the others because I loved her very much and endured with her her labors and pains. Besides these duties given me by our Lord, I had other sick to care for; besides, I had charge of the pantry and was assistant in the kitchen. These different employments obliged me to do during the night what was necessary for our holy Mother. I reserved the day for the service of the other religious.

One day, during Mass, I experienced pain in my soul; from this pain I entered into a supernatural recollection, and whilst I was in this state our Lord appeared to me under the form of the *Ecce Homo*, as He was when Pilate presented Him to the people, crowned with thorns, His hands bound, a rope about His neck, and His whole body covered with wounds; the clamorous cries of the Jews, "Crucify Him! Crucify Him!" rang in my head. The Divine Master approached me and said to me lovingly: "My daughter, see the condition I am in. Do you think your sufferings can compare with Mine?" These words pierced my heart like arrows and caused me to be so inflamed with love that I felt filled with courage to endure for the future much greater sufferings. This vision passed away quickly, and I remembered what our Lord had formerly told me: that I would have much to suffer. I was delivered of the weakness that caused me to complain of little pains, and found strength in the remembrance of the vision when the Divine Master had told me that I would have much to suffer in company with the Saint.

As for her, subject as she was to many infirmities, she suffered extremely during her journeys; her sufferings greatly outweighed mine. But I shared all hers and experienced a pain that I knew not how to express, when in the inns I could find scarcely anything necessary for the relief of this holy Mother.

Another time, while at the Convent of St. Joseph of Avila, on Wednesday in Holy Week, I was thinking of the sufferings which would overwhelm our Lord during His Passion. My soul became recollected, and during this recollection the Divine Master appeared to me as a man who takes to flight because they wish to capture him and enters the door of a friend's house. It was thus that He entered my soul. But His countenance was extremely troubled, as that of a man who turns to see who is about to arrest him. He did not address me a single word. I felt so afflicted that I said to Him: "Lord, what willest Thou? Here is my heart, enter it." But, without saying anything, He went out, leaving me full of grief at the sight of His affliction.

When our holy Mother held Chapter, the Divine Master was often pleased to console us. It seemed to us as if we were in heaven, and the Saint was sometimes resplendent with glory.

CHAPTER VIII

JOY IN TENDING ST. TERESA

Sufferings of St. Teresa and Her Companion in Their Journeys—Extraordinary Sufferings Endured at Burgos During the Inundation of That City; Miraculous Help—With What Charity and Joy Anne Cared for St. Teresa Until Her Last Sigh.

I will return to the sufferings we endured in our journeys. This is what occurred at the foundation of Villanueva de la Jara. We had no other water but that drawn from a very deep well. One day, when the Saint was having a windlass constructed in order to draw the water more easily, she went out to look at it; the workman forgot to fasten the windlass and it commenced to turn. As God loved the Saint, He wished to give her occasion for merit. The handle struck the sore arm and wounded it again. A few days after an abscess formed on it, and so serious was it that if God had not granted the favor of leaving her with us a little longer there would have been no remedy for it. We were expecting her death when the abscess broke. This martyrdom of the Saint was like death for all her daughters, and for me in particular.

If I were obliged to recount all the sufferings she had to endure during the years that I was with her, I would never finish. What she tells in her writings is nothing in comparison with the reality. The account of the foundation of Burgos, which was the last, depicts only a very small part of what she suffered there. And what poverty! The necessaries of life were wanting to us. I recall one day, when the Saint was extremely weak, I had nothing to give her but a little bread soaked in water. The river had overflowed to such an extent that the inhabitants of Burgos could not aid us, and for our part we could not send out anyone on any account, our house being far from the city and on the bank of the river. The water rose to such a height that it flooded our monastery, and, as it was an old building, at each motion of the river it shook as if about to fall. The Saint's room was so poor that the light from the sky could be seen through the roof; the walls were full of cracks, and it was exceedingly cold, for the climate at Burgos is very severe. The river rose to the first floor of our house. Seeing our danger, we hastened to have the Blessed Sacrament carried to the highest part of the building, and each succeeding hour we thought we should be drowned. We began to recite Litanies. From six in the morning until midnight we were in this peril without eating or without a moment's repose. Our only fear was that our holy Mother would perish in the water before our eyes. As for her, she was the most afflicted person in the world. She had just founded the house, and our Lord left her so alone that she knew not what was best to do, whether to remain quietly in the

Life of Blessed Anne of St. Bartholomew

monastery or to go out, as so many other religious had done from theirs. During this time we were all so anxious that we never thought of giving anything to our holy Mother. It was quite late when she said to me: "My daughter, see if there is any bread left; give me a mouthful; I feel very weak." This broke my heart. But what could I do? The bread was under water; we sent a novice who was strong down into it; it reached to her waist; finally she found the bread, and we gave a little of it to our holy Mother, for we had nothing else. And if some sailors had not brought us help, we would have perished; but it really seemed as if these sailors were God's angels. We did not know how they came, nor how they entered under the water and broke in the doors of the house, so that the water began to recede from the rooms; but they had been so submerged, and filled with so many stones, that more than eight carts were necessary to carry away what the water had brought in. Our holy Mother's apartment, as I have already said, shook and seemed on the point of falling. It was so rickety that the night air could easily have caused our Mother's death. I had two coverings on my bed. I stretched one above her head during the night and the other around her bed; I did it in such a way that she did not perceive it, for if she had seen that I was depriving myself she would never have permitted it. As soon as she fell asleep, I would gently draw near and seat myself beside her bed. When she would call me I would act as if coming from my cell, and the Saint would say: "My daughter, how is that you came so quickly?" At other times, seeing that she slept, I would go out to wash her linen; as she was sick it was a consolation to me to give her clean clothing, for she greatly loved neatness. Many nights I passed without closing my eyes, but I did not feel the loss of sleep. So happy was I to give her pleasure, and this great happiness that I experienced lasted until her death. The day she died she could not speak. I changed all her linen, headdress and sleeves, and she looked at herself, quite satisfied to see herself so clean; and, turning her eyes towards me, she looked at me smilingly, and showed her gratitude by signs.

To return to what I was saying [about the foundation at Burgos], I felt as strong and my mind as peaceful as if I had slept entire nights and had been delicately nourished. Our Lord did this for the consolation of the Saint, for if she had noticed that the work injured my health it would have caused her much pain. God, for love of His friend, worked this miracle as well as others in a miserable sinner like myself. I did not deserve to serve her; therefore, I lived in great fear of having profited so little by such a grace. And I had great reason to fear, for when still very young I loved very much to play and recreate with other little girls of my own age, and when I had some scruple I would say to our Lord: "My Lord, if I had the happiness of living with a Saint I would be better, I would do what I saw her do, and would take pattern by her example." Owing to these thoughts I would be

38

covered with confusion returning from play. If it pleased the Divine Master to grant me such a grace, it was not because of my desires; truly it can easily be believed that these desires did not come from me, but from Him. He had already in His wisdom and mercy arranged all, disposed of all, and He inspired me with this desire in order that when finally finding myself in this holy company, and for all that not performing my duty, I would be overwhelmed at having been so proud and vain as to desire a favor of which I was not worthy, and from which I did not profit as another would have done in my place.

CHAPTER IX

DEPARTURE FOR ALBA

Departure From Burgos for Alba—New Sufferings of St. Teresa During the Journey—Charity of Anne of St. Bartholomew—Heroic Patience of the Saint.

I will return to the sufferings which the Saint endured in her journeys. After all she had been obliged to endure in the foundation of the Monastery of Burgos, our Lord said to her: "You may go on; sufferings have not been wanting to you here, but there remain still others for you to endure." The prediction of the Divine Master was verified; from Burgos to Alba the route was one chain of sufferings for the Saint. At Vallodolid, where she stopped to find a little repose, she found only an increase of pain; the Divine Master gave her part of His cross to beautify her crown. On leaving Vallodolid she went to Medina-del-Campo; this was on the way to the Monastery of Avila, of which she was Prioress. The very evening of our arrival at Medina, she had a recommendation to make the Prioress regarding something which was not done as it should be. In order to increase her merit, God permitted that the Prioress should take this counsel in very bad part. The Saint was deeply grieved; she retired to one apartment and the Prioress to another. The Saint experienced such intense pain on account of what had taken place, that she passed the night without eating or sleeping. In the morning we left without receiving any provision for the journey, and yet the Saint was already ill with the sickness of death. During that whole day I could find nothing to give her to eat. The following day, having reached a little hamlet, we found ourselves in the same poverty; there was absolutely nothing to eat, and the Saint was extremely weak. She said to me: "My child, give me something, for I feel very badly." I had only some dry figs, and the Saint was burning with fever. I gave some one four reals to find me two eggs, no matter at what price. When I found that with money they had not been able to find anything and they returned my reals, I could not look at the Saint without weeping, for she appeared like one half dead. The sorrow I experienced on this occasion was beyond words to express. It seemed to me that my heart would break, and I did nothing but weep in my exceeding pain to see her dying, and to be unable to find anything to relieve her. She said to me with angelic patience: "Do not weep, my child! God wishes it so now." As she drew near her happy passage to the eternal life, our Lord tried her in every way; but she accepted it as she always did, that is to say, like a Saint. But I suffered greatly, being less mortified than she. It was necessary that the Saint should console me; therefore she said: "Do not be troubled at all; I am satisfied with the fig I have just eaten."

40

CHAPTER X

LAST MOMENTS OF ST. TERESA

Their Arrival at Alba—Sickness and Last Moments of St. Teresa—The Care Lavished Upon Her by Her Faithful Companion Notwithstanding the Excess of Her Grief—The Last Day, the 4th of October, the Saint Enters Into Ecstasy at Seven in the Morning and Remains in It Until Nine in the Evening, Her Head Resting on the Heart and Supported by the Arms of Anne of St. Bartholomew—At Nine O'Clock Anne Saw Jesus Christ Come to Seek Her and Her Soul Fly Like a Dove to Heaven—Return of Anne of St. Bartholomew to Avila.

The day after our arrival at Alba, she was so greatly exhausted that the physicians feared, for the moment, that she could not live: a great sacrifice for me, the greater because I must remain in this world. For, aside from the love I bore her and that she had for me, I had another great consolation in her company: almost continually I saw Jesus Christ in her soul and the manner in which He was united to it, as if it was His heaven. This knowledge filled me with the deep reverence one should feel in the presence of God. Truly it was heavenly to serve her, and the greatest torture was to see her suffer. I spent about fourteen years with her. Immediately, when I entered to receive the habit, she took me into her cell, and during the rest of her life I was always with her, except during her journey to Seville; for then, as has already been said, I was sick at Avila. And these fourteen years seemed to me less than one day. The Saint, for her part, was so accustomed to my poor and awkward service, that she would not be without me. She showed this very plainly in the following circumstance: I fell sick with a fever the very eve of the day when she was to leave for the visitation of her monasteries. I was not at all in a condition to undertake the journey. She said to me: "Do not be disturbed, my child! I shall leave orders here to send you to me as soon as the fever leaves you." But at midnight, when she sent a religious to ask how I was, I found that I was free from fever. She rose from her bed, came to me, and said: "It is true, my daughter, you no longer have any fever; we can easily undertake the journey. I hope it may be so, and I will recommend the matter to God." And so it was; we left in the morning. During the five days preceding her death at Alba, I was more dead than alive. Two days before her death, she said to me once when we were alone: "My child, the hour of my death has come." This pierced my heart more and more. I did not leave her for a moment. I begged the religious to bring me what was necessary for her. I gave it to her. It was a consolation to her for me to do so. The day of her death she was unable to speak from early morning: in the evening, the Father who was attending her (Father Anthony of Jesus, one of the two first Discalced Carmelites) told me to go take some nourishment. But scarcely

41

Life of Blessed Anne of St. Bartholomew

had I left than the Saint became restless; with an anxious air she looked from one side to the other. The Father asked her if she wished me near her. She answered yes, by signs. They called me; I hastened back. As soon as she saw me, she smiled at me, showed me such condescension and affection that she caught me with her two hands and rested her head in my arms. I held her thus in my embrace until she expired, being more dead than the Saint herself; for, as for her, she was so inflamed with love for her Spouse that she sighed for the moment of parting from her body in order to be with Him.

As our Lord is so good and saw how little patience I had to bear this cross, He appeared to me at the foot of the Saint's bed in all His Majesty, accompanied by His blessed ones who came to seek her soul. This glorious vision lasted the space of a Credo, giving me time to exchange my pain and grief for a great resignation, to ask pardon of our Lord and say to Him: "My Lord, even should Your Majesty wish to leave her for my consolation, I would ask You, now that I have witnessed Your glory, not to leave her one moment in this exile." Scarcely had I uttered these words than she expired, and this blessed soul soared like a dove to enjoy the possession of her God.

As the Saint loved me so much, I had begged her to console me, and to ask of our Lord for me perfect liberty of spirit, without attachment for anyone whomsoever. I was naturally affectionate, and I loved the Saint more than anyone could love her, also the other religious whom I saw advanced in perfection and loved by the Saint. I loved them very much; and sometimes the Saint told me this attachment for friends was not good for my soul, and I must overcome it for my spiritual welfare; but until that hour when God called her to Himself, I had not succeeded. It was she who obtained this grace for me, for from that time I was free and detached and it seemed to me that I had a yet greater love for the religious, loving them without any mixture of self-love; and, for the rest, it was as if I were alone in the world. I love all my Sisters in God and for God. I received such strength of soul to prepare the body of the Saint for burial, that I did it with as much calmness as if her death had been a matter of indifference to me.

I wished to remain in that convent, but neither the Superior nor the religious of the Monastery of Avila, to which I belonged, would give their consent. They sent for me in haste. I felt some perplexity of soul. But the Saint appeared to me and said: "My daughter, obey the command given you, and depart!"

CHAPTER XI

HER DEVOTION TO ST. TERESA

Her Devotion to St. Teresa—She is Carried by Angels to the Tomb of the Saint at Alba—They Show Her the Body Miraculously Preserved—Translation of the Holy Body to the Monastery of Avila—Favors Received by Anne of St. Bartholomew From the Saint.

From the time of my return to the Convent of Avila, I prayed to the Saint and recommended myself to her. I spoke of this to my confessor. He told me it was wrong to recommend myself to a Saint who was not yet canonized and commanded me not to do it. That same night whilst asleep, the Saint appeared to me most glorious and resplendent. She said to me: "My child, ask of me anything you wish and I will obtain it for you." Awakening, then, I said to her: "I ask of you the Spirit of God, that it may always dwell in my soul." She disappeared, leaving me in perfect certainty of the opinion I had formed of her sanctity. The command of my confessor, however, did not fail to cause me pain, for he had told me not to pray to her as a Saint. Even had not the signal favors granted her by God, and which proved that He loved her, led me to think her such, the consideration alone of the love with which she had endured for God so many labors, of which I was witness, and in which I had taken some part, would cause me to state as a certainty that she was a real Saint.

I may add, that what our Lord had said to me was fulfilled; that in her company I would have great sufferings to share with her. I speak here of exterior sufferings; as for those which the Saint endured and which were not apparent, they were beyond measure.

I recall what happened to her one Christmas Eve; it was during the time of her great sufferings and persecutions. The Nuncio had given a permit authorizing the Calced Carmelites to take bodily possession of all the Discalced. In the evening they had brought her a letter in which she was informed that the Discalced Carmelites were to be suppressed and that the Nuncio wished their houses destroyed. Before going to Matins I begged her to take a little collation. Whilst she was in the refectory, our Lord approached her, cut the bread and put a piece in her mouth, saying to her: "My daughter, eat! I know that you suffer greatly, but take courage; it cannot be otherwise." That night, while at Matins, her eyes were like two fountains of tears, and we could not look at her without weeping as she did.

Her sufferings were such that we could not help feeling them intensely. There was not one in which I did not have a large share. As I loved her, and as I had had part in all her tribulations and sorrows, I was to share also her joys and felicity in heaven.

From the time in which she appeared to me in such great glory, as I have already narrated, I earnestly desired that her holy body

43

Life of Blessed Anne of St. Bartholomew

should be brought back to Avila. One day, occupied with this thought, and believing that they feared to remove the holy body because they knew not in what condition they would find it, I fervently begged of our Lord to make this known to me. Immediately I entered into a spiritual slumber, and angels carried me to the sepulcher; they opened it and showed me the body; it was entire, having the same color as when later they brought it forth from the tomb, and it exhaled the same odor and perfume. The angels showed me two sleeves on her arms, also entire and in the same condition as when I placed them there. They said: "Are you satisfied? Do you wish anything more?" I replied yes, that I would be more satisfied if I saw the Saint in her own convent at Avila, but that the Duke of Alba would never consent to it. They said to me: "Do not make any account of the opposition of the Duke of Alba. It is the king who will decide; this matter depends on him alone." The Duke and Duchess of Alba died soon after, and the king, to please his heirs, was unwilling that the holy body should be transferred to Avila. Before this happened, the Order earnestly desired the translation of the holy body from Alba to Avila. My tender affection for the Saint led me to recommend the affair to God with great fervor. Our Lord said to me: "Do not be troubled; the holy body will return to this house." Continuing with importunity, I asked our Lord when this would take place, because I was eager to know. He replied: "It will be on the Feast of the Presentation of the Blessed Virgin." There was still almost a year to wait; but on the day fixed the thing was accomplished; they took the body of the Saint from the house at Alba and transferred it to that of Avila. It was received there with the liveliest transports of joy. The number of lights burning was so great the convent seemed like a heaven. The Saint gave a thousand proofs of tenderness towards her children; in whatever part of the convent they might be, she appeared to them and consoled them.

One day I spoke to my confessor of one of my soul's secrets, and he did not take it well; he said to me: "That sounds to me like Mother Teresa; go on now, do not be like her, let those things alone." It seemed to me that he pronounced these words with but little esteem for our holy Mother. I was grieved because of this, and sought a solitary spot in the garden. There, deeply pained at the thought that the Saint was not appreciated as she deserved, I began to pray. Soon I entered a state of supernatural recollection, and in this state saw the Divine Master approaching me under the form He had when living in this world. He was robed in a most brilliant pontifical cope. When near me He raised one side of the cope—it was the side next to His Heart—and showed me the Saint resplendent in glory; He held her on His arm, as if she were no longer anything but a part of Himself, and said to me: "Behold her, I have brought her to you here; be not at all troubled; let them say what they will." After these words He disappeared. I felt within my soul a profound recollection and deeper fervor at the sight of the love God bore the Saint.

44

Her Devotion to St. Teresa

On another occasion I begged the holy Mother to obtain for me from God the favor of knowing which of the virtues was most agreeable to Him, for I was impelled to make every effort to acquire it; one day she appeared to me and said: "My child, it is humility."

Very often the holy Mother strengthened me by a sentiment of love and by a heavenly odor of which I was as conscious as if I had been near her holy body. And though she did not show herself, I was aware of this perfume and the favor she did me in keeping near me. I will give a very striking example: Once I was overcome with fatigue; all the religious were ill, there was only one Sister and myself able with difficulty to keep on our feet and to wait on ourselves. I went to the tomb of the Saint and said to her: "Mother, come to my aid; see me here before you, my body so crushed with fatigue that I cannot keep up. Give me strength; I desire it only to serve all my Sisters." I felt the conviction that she heard me and that she said to me: "Go, my child, I will do what you have asked of me." I went to the kitchen and scarcely had I commenced to stir the embers than I noticed the perfume of the Saint, as if she were there; there came forth from the ashes an odor similar to that exhaled by her holy body; this odor communicated such strength to my body that not the slightest trace of fatigue remained. My body had no more feeling than if it had been a spirit. There was not a shadow of lassitude, and this supernatural strength continued with me until all the religious had recovered health. Very often the pans and everything I touched in the kitchen exhaled the odor of the relic of her holy body; it was something marvelous; one would have declared that she, herself, had touched these objects with her hands.

CHAPTER XII

REVELATION REGARDING SPREAD OF THE ORDER

First Revelation of Her Journey to France—The Divine Master Makes
Known to Her at Different Times What is His Will Regarding This—
Uselessness of Their Efforts to Detain Her in Spain.

During the foundation of Ocagna, Christmas Eve after Matins
I entered into deep recollection. During this spiritual slumber
there was placed before my eyes my journey to France. I beheld
myself on a dark sea, with companions who were all, with one
exception, unknown to me. The effect of this vision was very
great. I had often before felt a keen desire for martyrdom, but
these desires, always accompanied by some fear, were far from
being as perfect as those I experienced now, for I accepted martyrdom for God's sake, not only with entire conformity of will and
with joy, but also with a more intense love than I have ever felt
when thinking of giving my life for God.

Since this vision I have always had present to my mind that
what God had shown me He willed to be my cross. But as the
flesh was fearful, our Lord appeared to me one day in an intellectual vision; I realized that He was present, but did not see Him;
He said to me: "The olive and the grape must pass through the
press of martyrdom to yield their liquor; it is by this way all My
friends walk." He added: "It is thus that I would have Thee"
—and He disappeared. This vision excited within me new courage,
for before that I was cast down. Taking heart once more, I offered
myself again for all that God wished of me; with all the sincerity
of which I was capable I placed my heart in His hands, and I felt
that my determination was pleasing to Him.

One day, after Communion, I was thinking of what a priest
had said to me, that it was neither expedient nor necessary that
religious women should go to France in the midst of so many heretics; that it was not for them to preach to them. As these words
seemed to me true, our Lord appeared to me and said: "Pay no
attention to what they have said to you: just as flies seek a drop
of honey, so will you attract souls." This happened when the
French were making most earnest efforts in Spain to obtain Spanish nuns. Opinions were greatly divided on this point. As all
those who had taken up the affair were learned men and great
servants of God, those who doubted made me hesitate and wonder
if it was God who spoke to me; but my confessors reassured
me, declaring that it was God, and they gave me courage. The
prospect of change of country, and these doubts which disturbed
me, afflicted me greatly, though I had but one desire, that of knowing God's will and doing what would be most agreeable to Him.
As my heart was beaten by this tempest of doubt, God made known
His will to other souls in order to dissipate my fears. A very

46

Revelation Regarding Spread of the Order

holy religious in our monastery did not approve of my departure, and earnestly desired to see this plan abandoned. She said to the Divine Master: "How can you wish this Sister to go so far away?" Our Lord replied to her that it must be so, and that it was not good to wish anything else. When she replied, that she feared all that this Sister would have to suffer, the Divine Master said to her: "Those who take honey away from the hives are stung, but they carry away the honey."

All the religious of St. Joseph at Avila and all the inhabitants of the city recommended me to God. Everyone feared to see me leave for a strange country filled with heretics. In the convent the sorrow was general, for it was a house of God in which all the religious loved one another, and they were extremely fond of me, without my having in any way merited it. For my part, I loved them very much, because they were holy souls.

CHAPTER XIII

PRAYERS FOR SALVATION OF FRANCE

Many Souls in France, Like Moses, Raise Their Hands to Heaven for the Salvation of That Nation—For This End They Desire to Have the Daughters of St. Teresa.

The Carmelites of Avila, as I have said, made every effort to prevent the Superiors from authorizing my departure, but it was useless because Divine Providence had from all eternity decreed that I should go. There is no country in the world so abandoned that God will not leave in it some Moses to pray for it with heart and hands raised to heaven. This is what we see in France. When that country seemed in greatest danger of losing its faith, God left there not one but many Moses to raise their arms in behalf of their people, and to obtain mercy by their watchings, their mortifications and their tears.

In this time of trial and desolation for the Catholics of France, there were to be found many among them who were very good and great servants of Jesus Christ. They knew that the great Teresa, the Mother of the Discalced Carmelites, had risen up with unsatiable zeal for the salvation of souls; that in order to labor efficaciously for their salvation, this virgin, sustained by grace and full of the spirit of God, had reformed her Order, bringing it back to the observance of the primitive rule, and establishing in it all possible austerity; they saw, too, that her determined object was, as she says in her writings, that all those who would join her monasteries should be always engaged in prayer and holy exercises of mortification and penance, in order to aid Jesus Christ and His Catholics in the conversion of the kingdom of France. This country was continually present to her thoughts, and she wished so earnestly for its salvation, that she did not cease to cry to God in order to obtain it. After having founded her first monastery of St. Joseph at Avila for this purpose, this Saint had founded many others of men as well as women, and when God called her to Himself, that she might enjoy the fruit of her labors, He left her Order in the form of a separate province. Finally, at her death and since, as God wished her to be known by the world, He glorified her by a great number of miracles.

At this time, there were in Spain several Frenchmen who longed for the salvation of their people, and for this purpose earnestly wished to have the daughters of St. Teresa in France. But the one to whom, amongst all the rest, God gave the palm, was one of His servants, a French priest named M. de Bretigny.

CHAPTER XIV

PROPHECY REGARDING MISSION

The Divine Master Once More Makes Known to Her That It is His Will She Should Leave for France—Prophecy Regarding Her Mission in That Country—Apparition of the Archangel St. Michael; He Encourages Her to Go Without Fear—Six Resplendent Stars Appear Over the Monastery of St. Joseph at Avila, and Are a Figure of the Six Spanish Carmelites Destined to Go to France.

Before the departure for France, our Lord spoke to another Sister in the Convent at Avila, and said to her: "Tell her to go and have no fears; I say to her as to My disciples, that she will be afflicted and despised, but her tribulations will be turned into joy." That which my Adorable Master said to my friends strengthened me more than what He had spoken to me.

Another day, suffering this same anxiety, I entered into a partly spiritual slumber. I then saw a young man of most noble bearing and armed as a warrior. He said to me: "Do not hesitate about leaving, and show some courage." From what I experienced in my soul, he who spoke to me was the Archangel St. Michael, to whom I had been devoted from my most tender years and to whom I prayed every day.

All those who were to form the little colony met in our Convent at Avila on the Feast of St. Bartholomew. We remained there until the Feast of the Beheading of St. John the Baptist. Before our departure and before the names of those who were to leave had been made known, there was seen in the heavens, for an entire month, very brilliant stars; they shone during the day as well as the night, and each one was larger than ordinary stars; they were a figure of those among us who were to leave for France, and I was the smallest of all.

Some time before the departure, while I was experiencing the interior combats of which I have spoken, our Lord said to me: "See how the birds fly to the birdlime. It is thus that souls will adhere to you, and they will be Mine forever."

THIRD BOOK

CHAPTER I

DEPUTATION SENT FROM FRANCE

Journey of M. de Bretigny to Spain, Several Years Before the Foundation of Carmel in Paris—He Tries, But in Vain, to Obtain Spanish Carmelites for France—Forced for the Time Being to Give Up His Plan, He Takes Away With Him the Writings of the Saintly Foundress and Has Them Translated Into French—The Reading of Them Increases the Desire of the French for the Daughters of St. Teresa—They Work for It Several Years; Finally Their Efforts Are Crowned With Success —Messrs. de Bretigny, de Berulle, René Gauthier, and Three French Ladies Go to Spain, and Take Back to France Six Spanish Carmelites.

Some years before our departure for France, M. de Bretigny made a journey to Spain. He begged most earnestly of the Superiors of the Order permission to take some Spanish Carmelites to France; but he could not then succeed in his design. Not having been able to get the Carmelites, he took home the writings of the Saint and had them translated into French. As in these works there is so much said in favor of France, the French servants of God who had devotion to our holy Foundress loved her more and more, and took new courage.

In several cities they gathered together some very virtuous high-born ladies to initiate them little by little into the spirit of this new Order. These reunions once well established, they asked permission of the king to found a monastery in Paris, desiring for this purpose to have Spanish Carmelites brought there; but in case the Carmelites were not willing, their plan was to have our Constitutions brought from Spain and be taught to these young ladies whom they had gathered together, with the intention of giving them the habit and making them daughters of the Order of our Holy Mother, St. Teresa.

This first foundation having been arranged, the servant of God whom I mentioned above, M. de Bretigny, returned to Spain, bringing with him three noble French ladies. They intended, if their enterprise was successful, to take Spanish religious with them to France. Besides, during their stay in Spain, they were to learn the language of the country. Messrs. René Gauthier and de Berulle also went to Spain, not without meeting great dangers at sea, as they themselves narrated. For our Lord tried their courage in every way and on all sorts of occasions. But they were so faithful to God and so firm in their design, that nothing terrified them. They were several months in Spain without succeeding in obtaining religious from the Order. Seeing this, M. de Berulle and the others did their utmost and labored for a whole year before obtaining from the Superiors of the Order what they asked. They

Deputation Sent From France

had to endure much labor and many affronts; this, because it was not known what great servants of God they were; for they certainly were such—their works and the zeal they showed for the glory of God proved their great fervor. But in order that their virtue might be more purified, God permitted that they should not be esteemed at their proper worth. Some said that they were heretics, and other things of a similar nature. They suffered with much patience and humility, and, persevering in this way, their enterprise was crowned with success.

CHAPTER II

JOURNEY TO FRANCE

The Little Colony Leaves Avila on the Twenty-Ninth of August, Feast of the Beheading of St. John the Baptist, and Sets Out for France—Particulars of the Journey.

At last our Father General, Francis of the Mother of God, came to Avila with several Fathers of the Order to arrange for our departure. We left on the morning of the Feast of the Beheading of St. John the Baptist. Our Father General accompanied us a great part of the day. When he was obliged to leave us we begged his blessing. He gave it with an emotion that was shared by all the religious. In parting, both Fathers and daughters made a great sacrifice to God.

Two friars of our Order, great servants of God, two French priests, one of whom was M. de Berulle, and the other, M. René Gauthier, together with three Frenchmen on horseback, and several Spaniards, accompanied us on this journey. The three French ladies were alone in one carriage and the six religious in another. We were together in the inns. The French ladies taught us their language; it must be acknowledged we did not make great progress in it; we learned sufficient, however, to understand most of what was said to us. But we did not speak fluently; we could, with difficulty, say only a few sentences. Our Lord wished to humble us in this, and I think it was best for us, for by speaking little we did not give disedification. Every nation has its own customs.

We proceeded happily on our journey; but the devil, seeing how his plots might be ruined by our undertaking, commenced, our Lord so permitting, to try us by accidents and most painful fatigue. I will leave you to judge what poor women must have suffered in so long a journey; think, above all, what it must have cost poor religious—I say nothing of being obliged to go on foot—but to be exposed to the gaze of passers-by, and obliged to accept the assistance of the first-comer, to be helped in places over precipices, or out of the deep mire. I cannot think of all these dangers even now, without shivering with fear.

But I know not how to give sufficient and well-deserved praise to our French companions for the unceasing care they took of us, and for the virtue they constantly manifested. They treated us with so much respect, their conduct was so perfect, that we felt under the greatest obligations to them, and were filled with confusion. During all that long journey, not an improper or impatient word was heard, not even were those little pleasantries permitted which are usually made use of to lighten the weariness and fatigue of journeying. For this I praise God; I appreciated their virtue and

Journey to France

holiness; I was charmed with the respect they showed to the habit of the Blessed Virgin and our holy Mother Teresa.

Before reaching Bayonne, there was one day when the rain fell in such torrents that neither the driver of our carriage nor those on horseback could be of any help to us. On this occasion the good Master wished to try the patience of His servants. Night surprised us on a high mountain, and it was so dark we could not see our hand before us. Here we were obliged to remain, without any other shelter. It was the eve of the Feast of St. Mathew, and we had all forgotten it. God willed we should be in so great want that we had neither bread, wine nor water, except what was falling from the skies; it fell in such abundance one would have thought it was being poured on us by the bucketful. The wind was so great it seemed as if everything would be overturned. The sea near by could be heard roaring frightfully. Under other circumstances I would have feared greatly, but during the entire journey my soul was almost continually in the presence of her Spouse; from this I received great consolations and favors, and a peace and tranquillity which were surely from heaven. Once only was this calm disturbed. I was saddened at the thought that I was of so little use, a simple lay-Sister, and would be a burden instead of a help to the Order. But the Divine Master appeared to me fastened to the cross and full of love for my soul; He consoled me and said: "My daughter, be of good courage; I will help you and be with you." From that moment I experienced neither pain nor interior desolation. I felt, so it seemed to me, that the whole world already belonged to me, and that I was like a queen; enjoying a great sense of liberty in my soul. I felt real consolation at the sight of the little humiliations to which I might be obliged to submit in this world for the love of my God. All during the journey my soul enjoyed the presence of the Most Holy Trinity to such a degree that neither the many dangers nor any possible accident could deprive me of it; I was constantly recollected in prayer.

That same day we crossed a bridge which spanned a great river. Scarcely had we reached the middle than the evil spirit attempted to throw us into the river to be engulfed in the water. Suddenly the mules took fright and the coach was raised up in the air on one side. Seized with fear at this sight, my companions cried out to God, and the coach crossed the bridge only to be overturned a little farther on. It could be easily seen that it was the work of the demon, for scarcely had we left the bridge than we were upset in a ditch filled with thorns and briars. I was seated next the door; the coach fell on this side and all my companions fell on me. All present cried out and said, speaking of me: "She is dead!" However, I felt neither the sting of the thorns, nor any painful shock; it was as if God had held me in His arms. Whilst buried under the others, I heard someone crying aloud and knew not the cause. I soon learned that one had received a wound in the foot and another in the eye. It was necessary to

53

call the surgeon of the place to dress their wounds. They were brave women and God treated them as such; as I was nothing and good for nothing, our Lord spared me.

CHAPTER III

ARRIVAL IN FRANCE

Reception Given the Spanish Carmelites in France—Foundation of the First Monastery, the 18th of October, 1604—First French Novices—Some Remarks Concerning Andreé Levoix.

COMMENTARY

From the Pyrenees to the capital of France the journey was pleasant. At Bordeaux, Saintes, Poitiers and Orleans, the Spanish Carmelites were received with the greatest honor and profound respect. M. de Berulle had gone in advance from Bayonne to announce to the king the approach of the colony. The court was at Fontainebleau. Henry IV received M. de Berulle kindly, and charged him to recommend himself and his kingdom to the prayers of the Spanish Carmelites. Learning the day of their intended arrival in Paris, M. de Berulle and M. de Marillac preceded them to Longjumeau. When they joined the pious colony, they walked at its head towards the capital, which they entered about the 15th of October, 1604; later, this day was consecrated to God as the Feast of St. Teresa.

As they entered Paris by the gate of the Faubourg Saint Jacques, they soon reached the priority of Notre Dame des Champs, which was to be the first monastery. However, they did not think well to stop here on their arrival. As it was the octave of the Feast of St. Denis, they thought it would be only right to visit the spot which possessed the relics of this illustrious Apostle of the capital and was sanctified by his martyrdom. They therefore set out on their way to Saint Denis. When they were on the bridge of Notre Dame, two carriages joined those of the Spanish religious; the Duchess de Longueville, foundress of the first monastery, and her sister, the Princess d'Estouteville were in the first; the Marchioness de Breaute, Mme. Acarie* and her three daughters were in the second. As soon as they left the capital, they alighted to greet one another, and this greeting was made to the great satisfaction of both parties. They then re-entered their carriages and started for St. Denis, where they visited the church and the relics of the Abbey. The Carmelites, as well as the cortege which accompanied them from Paris, returned to the capital. Mme. Acarie did not sleep that night; she was preoccupied with the thought of the blessings God had showered on the new-born Order.

The following day, the 16th of October, the ladies who had conducted the Spanish Carmelites to St. Denis went with Mlle. de Fonteines-Marans to meet the religious and take them to Mont-

---

* Afterwards a Carmelite, and beatified as Blessed Mary of the Incarnation.

Life of Blessed Anne of St. Bartholomew

martre, a village quite near Paris. M. de Bretigny said Mass in the Chapel of the Martyrs and gave Holy Communion to all present. Then they visited the Benedictine Monastery. The Abbess gave Mother Anne of Jesus and her companions a most gracious welcome, and wished them to sleep in her house. Madame Jourdain availed herself of this occasion to see her daughter, who was eighteen years of age and had made her vows in this Abbey; she saw her then for the last time, as fifteen days later she took the religious habit in the first Carmelite Convent.

The following morning the Duchess of Longueville joined the Spanish Carmelites at Montmartre and conducted them to the Priority of Notre Dame des Champs. As soon as they entered, Mother Anne of Jesus, after the custom of St. Teresa in her foundations, intoned the Psalm *"Laudate Dominum,"* which was continued by her companions, and Sister Anne of St. Bartholomew went immediately to the kitchen to perform the duties of a lay-Sister and prepare dinner for the community.

The people came in crowds to Notre Dame des Champs to see the Carmelites take possession of their monastery; distinguished persons also assisted in great numbers at this touching ceremony. All praised God for the new Order of religious that had been established, returned thanks to Spain for the present she had made to France in giving Saints for foundresses..

After the Spanish religious had taken possession of the priority, they examined the interior arrangements. They could not sufficiently admire the genius of Mme. Acarie, who had known how, in so small a space, to make all the proper arrangements, together with all that was necessary for a community. They then visited the new buildings which were on the other side of the church; and the way in which this intelligent woman had grouped them seemed to them equally admirable.

Though the 17th of October, the day on which the Carmelites took possession of the convent, fell on Sunday, the Office was not chanted in their church on that day. The Cardinal of Gondy, Bishop of Paris, did not, until the following day, the 18th, send his first chaplain to bless in his name the religious, sing Mass and expose the Blessed Sacrament in their church. He gave the convent the name of the Incarnation. Three days later Queen Marie de Medicis visited the convent with the princesses and other ladies of the court; M. de Berulle presented M. de Bretigny to her. The queen showed the greatest kindness to the Spanish religious, and bestowed considerable alms on the house.

To complete the work of the foundation, there was only one thing to be done: that was, to receive novices into the convent. The postulants of the little congregation of St. Genevieve, which Mme. Acarie had formed two years previously for Carmel, sighed for the moment of entering, and there was not one among them who did not desire to be of the number of the first received. During the remainder of the month of October they were occupied with this important affair. As the Spanish religious did not understand the French language, they left the choice of the novices to their superiors. These last had until then had recourse to Mme. Acarie when there was question of admitting or refusing subjects who presented themselves for the little congregation. They now told her to choose among the postulants of this congregation those who would be the first to take the religious habit. It was then the Spanish Carmelites began to recognize this holy woman's gift in the discernment of spirits. It was resolved to admit at first only three persons; Mlle. de Fonteines-Marans was to be first of the three. The Spanish religious had received a favorable account of her vocation and her virtues. But they were obliged to postpone her reception, as her father was struck with a sudden illness, when he saw that his daughter was about to enter Carmel. Another was therefore taken to complete the number fixed upon. Mlle. d'Hannivel, Madame Jourdain and Andreé Levoix, of whom we have often spoken, were the three first novices chosen.

Mother Anne of Jesus fixed the day of their clothing for the Feast of All Saints. That it might be done with greater pomp, the Duchess de Longueville was asked to accompany Mlle. d'Hannivel; the Princess d'Estouteville, Madame Jourdan; and Madame Acarie, Andreé Levoix. Mlle. d'Hannivel was to receive the habit first of the three, but Providence arranged the precedence otherwise, and the disposition He made was followed. When the door of the convent was opened, Mother Anne of Jesus, instead of taking Mlle. d'Hannivel, went directly to Andreé Levoix and led her in with her companions. These last, through a spirit of humility, asked that this arrangement should not be disturbed; their request was granted, and Andreé Levoix became the first novice of the Order. The Provincial of the Carmelite Friars of Catalonia performed the ceremony of clothing the three novices; he had been invited to do so to honor him before returning to his own country. M. Gallemant, as first Superior, delivered the sermon. He took as text that part of the Scripture where Elias, after clothing Eliseus with his mantle, communicates to him his spirit. He spoke with much unction of the excellence of the religious habit, and of a vocation to so holy a state as that of a reformed Carmelite. Andreé Levoix was called Andreé of All Saints; Mlle. d'Hannivel, Mary of the Trinity, and Madame Jourdain, Louise of Jesus.

M. de Fonteines-Marans soon recovered from the illness brought on by his daughter's decision. He then immediately made to God the sacrifice of his dear child, and took her, himself, to the convent on the 11th of November. That same day she received the religious habit with Mlle. Deschamps; they gave to the first the name of Magdalen of St. Joseph; and to the second, Aimeé of Jesus. The 21st of the same month, the same ceremony was performed for Madame du Coudray; and they called her Mary of the Trinity, although Mlle. d'Hannivel bore that name. Finally on the 8th of the following December the habit was given to the Marchioness de Breauté, whom we have mentioned several times, and called her Mary of Jesus.

Life of Blessed Anne of St. Bartholomew

These were the first seven novices of the Carmel of France. All were an honor to their Order by the practise of religious virtues; and the greater number among them extended it by the foundation of several convents with which they were respectively charged.

CHAPTER IV

DUTY TO BECOME A CHOIR SISTER

The Blessed Mother Anne of St. Bartholomew is Raised From the Rank of a Lay-Sister to That of a Choir-Sister.

It pleased the Divine Master to continue granting me in Paris the favors and interior consolations of the journey.

Immediately after entering the new monastery, with the permission of the Prioress I went immediately to the kitchen to prepare some refection for the community. I did it with great pleasure; as I had always found my happiness in my position and in the duties of a lay-Sister. It is true, during her life, the holy Mother wished me to receive the black veil and proposed it to me several times, but I refused, saying that it would cause me much pain to give up my vocation. So she did not insist, because in all things she sought my happiness rather than her own. This was a great mortification to me, but my self-love made me believe that what I wished was more perfect, and that I had done well in resisting the holy Mother.

Our Superiors soon determined to oblige me to receive the black veil. This caused new trouble and conflict in my soul, not less painful than on preceding occasions. I feared having been at fault in refusing to please the holy Mother by not accepting from her hands what was now to be forced on me by strangers. The Prioress opposed this change, fearing such an example would cause relaxation in the Order in France and Spain. I was alone, and, as may be imagined, harassed with great fears. The Superiors said that on the contrary this example would have no unhappy consequences, that I must take the veil, and that the Spanish Father General had instructed them to do this after our arrival. All my companions were opposed to the decision of the Superiors, except Mother Eleanor of St. Bernard, who, during the journey, was always of this opinion. She consoled me on this occasion and certainly I had need of it. Several days passed in this way; the Mother Prioress remained firm in her way of considering it and the Superiors in theirs. While I was thus struggling against two opposing currents, Father Coton, S.J., visited our convent. Our Superiors had asked him to speak with me in order to persuade me to yield to their wishes. This Father, seeing that I was in great perplexity, said to me: "I, with all the Fathers in our house, will offer the Holy Sacrifice and make a novena, in order that God will enlighten us in this matter; and you will be bound in conscience to submit to what we judge to be the will of God."

During these nine days our Lord appeared to me two or three times and consoled me, which I needed greatly in the state I was in. In these apparitions, He was ravishingly beautiful; joy shone on His countenance, and He spoke to me with heavenly kindness.

Life of Blessed Anne of St. Bartholomew

Once He said to me in a sweet and loving manner: "Take courage, it cannot be otherwise." At the close of this novena, Father Coton came and asked me how I felt; I replied that I was in great pain; I said nothing to him of the favor our Lord had granted me, nor the consolations I had received from our holy Mother, for she also had appeared to me during this time. Father Coton told me that I was bound in conscience to obey, and added: "I believe that I can in the name of God command it in virtue of holy obedience, therefore, I do so; and you will sin if you do otherwise." He made known to the Superiors what he had said to me; it was their one desire, and finally I obeyed.

CHAPTER V

FOUNDATION OF MONASTERY OF PONTOISE

Foundation of the Monastery of the Carmelites of Pontoise—Blessed Mother
Anne of St. Bartholomew First Prioress of the Monastery.

No sooner was the first convent of the Carmelites founded in Paris than it was necessary to found others in several cities of the kingdom. The good odor of the virtues of the Spanish religious and the novices they formed spread far and wide, and caused the desire everywhere for Carmelite houses; the more so as the disorders of civil war had introduced relaxation into the greater number of other religious Orders. Madame Acarie, who had succeeded so well in establishing the first Carmelite Monastery in France, was then obliged to undertake the foundation of others of the same kind. We will mention them because of this holy woman's part in them.

It was a few days after the clothing of the first three novices, that they conceived the design of undertaking a new foundation. They found the priory, where they lived while waiting for the convent to be made habitable, was too small to accomodate all the subjects who were to be received, and the postulants who presented themselves desired ardently to receive the religious habit. Consequently, Blessed Mary of the Incarnation, then Mme. Acarie, and Mother Anne of Jesus made the proposal of a new foundation to the Superiors, and their idea was immediately accepted. To put it into execution, the Marquis of Breauté offered the sum of 10,000 crowns, and M. Duval his house in Pontoise. This house was then occupied by a community of young girls under the guidance of M. Gallemant, and several of them felt called to the life of Carmel. Then, too, Madame Acarie, who knew Pontoise, loved that city, because piety reigned there.

They charged this holy woman to inspect the house offered by M. Duval, and at the same time examine the young ladies of M. Gallemant's community who entertained the desire of becoming Carmelites.

M. d'Alincourt, a brother-in-law of the Marquis of Breauté and Governor of Pontoise, proposed to the inhabitants of the city the foundation contemplated, and they consented to it; the Cardinal of Bourbon, Archbishop of Rouen, also gave his consent to the foundation. In the meantime M. de Marillac took the necessary steps to obtain the letters patent from the king.

On the 10th of January, 1605, workmen were sent to the house destined for the Carmelites, and on the 25th of the same month it was ready for the reception of the religious. It was Blessed Mary of the Incarnation, who, on her return to Paris, arranged all the changes necessary in the building, and although she only slept one night in Pontoise, and was then principally occupied with

Life of Blessed Anne of St. Bartholomew

the examination of the young ladies who asked admission to Carmel, the condition of the place was so fixed in her mind, that she directed the changes in the best possible manner.

Sister Anne of St. Bartholomew, to whom they had just given the black veil, was named Prioress of the new monastery; Mother Isabel of the Angels, Sub-prioress; and Sister Beatrice of the Conception, Mistress of Novices. Mother Anne of Jesus, who governed the first convent, wished to accompany to Pontoise the three Spanish Carmelites sent there, and she took with her two of the first novices of the Order, Sister Louise of Jesus and Sister Aimée of Jesus.

They left Paris the 14th of January, 1605. Madame Acarie and her three daughters, M. de Berulle's mother, and several other ladies were in the party. Messrs. Gallemant, Duval and de Berulle joined it also, together with M. de Bretigny and M. Gauthier. The Duchess of Longueville and the Princess d'Estouteville accompanied the colony to St. Denis, as they were obliged to sleep there if they would communicate the following day on the tomb of the Apostle of the Capital.

On the 15th, after Mass, they set out for Pontoise. Before reaching it they stopped for several hours at Maubuisson, a celebrated Abbey of Bernardines, founded by the Mother of St. Louis in 1241. The religious of this Abbey received the Spanish Carmelites with reverence and made them presents.

The Provosts of Pontoise had come to Maubuisson in order to accompany the Carmelites to the house prepared for them. The Vicar General of Rouen awaited them there to install them, and everyone in the city, who had hastened to this ceremony, congratulated themselves on possessing persons so holy. After having taken possession of their monastery, the religious went to the refectory; and because of the respect she bore them, Madame Acarie wished to serve the table, notwithstanding all their endeavors to prevent it.

The Blessed Sacrament was not exposed in the church until the following day, which was Sunday, and the new convent was given the name of St. Joseph. The afternoon of that same day, three religious of Maubuisson, who had been edified by the sanctity which shone from the countenances of the Spanish Carmelites, begged to be admitted to the community. M. Duval was about to reply that it was contrary to the Constitutions of the Order to receive them, but Madame Acarie advised him not to give so prompt a reply in the negative. The thought of entering the Order of St. Teresa, she told him, would be very useful to these religious. Occupied with this intention, they will become very regular; whereas, if they are refused immediately, they will continue their ordinary way of life. This counsel was approved of and they followed it.

On Monday Mother Anne of Jesus gave the religious habit to four young ladies of M. Gallemant's community; the first received was called Agnes of Jesus; later she became Sub-Prioress, and took

Foundation of Monastery of Pontoise

great care of Blessed Mary of the Incarnation (Madame Acarie) in her last illness. After the ceremony, Mother Anne of Jesus, in order to excite the fervor of the novices just received, spoke these remarkable words: "You have entered an Order so holy and perfect, that by keeping its rules and constitutions faithfully, one will go directly from her deathbed to her home in heaven."

The first night these novices passed in the house they noticed a miraculous odor, which the Spanish Carmelites told them to call the perfume of St. Teresa.

On Tuesday they started on their return trip to Paris. They left Sister Louise of Jesus, who had to remain in the new monastery, at Pontoise. M. de Berulle remained there several days, to finish his advice to the community; and M. de Bretigny remained there seven or eight months in order to hear the confessions of the Spanish religious. On returning to Paris, Mother Anne of Jesus was in admiration of the way in which Madame Acarie had established the Order in France; and Madame Acarie admired the way in which Mother Anne of Jesus governed. The Carmelite said: "How could one woman have sufficient influence in France, Rome and Spain to make so difficult a foundation? How has she been able to find all the money used in it?" The Blessed one said in her turn: "How has a Spanish religious, who does not understand French, been able to acquire so much authority over persons of so different a language and customs? How has she been able to make them all one heart and one soul?"

The manuscript Annals of the Carmelites of Pontoise recount a very interesting anecdote, which occurred two years after the foundation of this monastery, that is to say, when they commenced building the new convent to which these religious were transferred in 1610, and where they have remained until the present day. This is the anecdote of which I have spoken.

The house given by M. Duval was small and in a poor situation; the number of subjects who presented themselves for admission increased every day. In 1607, therefore, they purchased a more spacious and convenient place. "But," said M. de Marillac, "though means for commencing the building were wanting, we did not trouble ourselves about that, Madame Acarie and I. This holy woman having expressed to me a great desire that the intended building should be commenced, I asked her if she thought God wished workmen should immediately undertake the work. She kept silence, and it seemed to me her wish was the result of some revelation made to her by the Holy Spirit, or some interior inspiration He had excited. I asked her a second time the same question, as I knew she was accustomed to wait until our Lord urged others to do something, rather than to urge it herself. She replied to me that God willed it. 'Do not speak any more of it,' I said, 'I will take charge of this affair.'" The workmen were immediately put to work; the building was finished in a few years; and, to the great astonishment of everyone, funds were never wanting. (Life of Blessed Mary of the Incarnation, by Boucher, Book III.)

CHAPTER VI

HONORS SHOWN THE CARMELITES

Honors Shown Blessed Mother Anne of St. Bartholomew and Her Companions by the Inhabitants of Pontoise—Assistance Given by Our Lord to His Servant in Governing This Monastery and Guiding Her Daughters.

The magistrates came to receive us half a mile outside the city. All the people arranged in procession welcomed us with demonstrations of most lively faith. The gathering was so great, and our entrance made with such solemnity, that we were unable to cross the threshold of our home until evening. There was reason to praise God in witnessing the devotion with which the inhabitants of Pontoise received this new foundation, and even now they retain the same sentiments. Our Lord has granted and ceases not to grant many favors to this city, owing to the prayers of the Sisters. Witnessing all this, I experienced intense sorrow only at the thought that I was to be head of the monastery. I was like one condemned to death, and so mortified that it seemed to me the office of Prioress, in my case, was a disgrace, and that never in any other circumstances had I been weighed down body and soul by such ignominy. My whole being seemed but a worm of the earth; and that in truth is what I am. But I never saw it in so clear a light as on that occasion.

Being one day before the Blessed Sacrament, I begged our Lord that He, Himself, would be watchful for His glory, and that He would assist me, as I felt entirely alone. He said to me: "I am here; I consider you as the light of my eyes."

Another day, I went to beg Him to be pleased to teach me what I should do, remembering I had no other Master. I was obliged to hold Chapter, and was greatly troubled on that account; this anxiety left me without strength and, as it were, unnerved at the thought of giving the necessary reproofs and instructions. Towards the end of Mass, which I heard in the convent, our Lord said to me: "Look at the Rule: it is there you will find the strength you need." With that I took courage and I went to hold Chapter. I spoke to the Sisters those things which God put in my mind to guide them in the beginning of their religious life. As regarded myself, I told them the truth, that notwithstanding my sincere desire to serve them, I considered myself very incapable; but that I trusted in God, in their virtue, and the desire they had so long entertained to see the Order of our holy Mother established in France; that our Lord would aid and satisfy them, in spite of the weakness of the instrument which He used. These words, and all that I said, were understood by the Sisters as if I had spoken their language, and as if they knew mine. When Chapter was over, I saw they were all weeping, and said to them: "No doubt

you are grieved because you do not understand my language."
They replied: "We have understood all that you said to us without the exception of one word, and this has caused us so great joy, that we weep with happiness."

These exercises of the religious life had just been established in our monastery at Pontoise, when they wrote me from Spain that God had called one of the religious to Himself, and that she had died like a Saint. I envied her, considering the great merit she must have acquired by the many labors she had borne during her life. Our Lord replied to me: "The better part is not for those persons who have the most active duties, but for those who die to themselves and to all their passions and inclinations."

Each time our Lord deigned to speak to me, although it passed so quickly, I received a great light, which made me understand more and more the goodness of God, and I felt interiorly a more intense desire to be faithful to Him. These words and visions of our Lord always reanimated my courage. But I had a great fear of my incapability, and dreaded becoming unfaithful to God. Since my arrival in this new monastery at Pontoise, I felt mortified beyond expression. It seemed to me that the Office of Prioress was for me a disgrace. I knew nothing regarding leading in the Choir. Every day I was with the novices and did not know their language. She who came as Sub-Prioress, Mother Isabel of St. Paul, taken from the house at Burgos, had chills and fever. I was the most worried woman in the world—so crushed it seemed nothing could humble me more, and that there was no sort of contempt comparable to seeing myself in this position, and so entirely incapable. I no longer knew myself, for usually my soul was full of courage. Often even our Lord gave me fortitude beyond that of woman, and now I had not sufficient to defend myself from a mouse, had it attacked me. It seemed to me I had never endured such pain, except at the death of our holy Mother. While in this state I felt her death intensely; I suffered at the thought of having survived her and being condemned to remain in this world without such a Mother and Mistress, without this living mirror of all the virtues which had been constantly before my eyes. Besides that, and not speaking of the love I bore her, I saw, aided by a light from God, Jesus Christ dwelling in her soul. I saw Him with great clearness and this almost constantly. From this privilege I derived astonishing strength, for being obliged to pass days and nights without finding any convenient time for prayer, and being obliged to take care of our Saint who had very little health and many occupations, I felt that my soul was always recollected in prayer; as to my body, it was as light as if it had not been. I did not feel its natural weight, and thought of nothing but performing what was commanded me.

CHAPTER VII

METHOD OF PRAYER

Her Manner of Prayer During Her Stay in the Monastery of Pontoise—
Graces and Lights She Received From Our Lord—Her Return to Paris.

The kind of prayer I practised at that time, on certain days, was a consciousness accompanied by deep reverence, of a light which was in my soul. All my faculties were so penetrated by it that they seemed to have no existence but that which they received from this light. It was not a vision of Jesus Christ as I saw Him usually, nor any other presence; but it was as if the Most Holy Trinity Itself dwelt in me; and though my soul perceived nothing, I felt for the Adorable Trinity the same reverence as if I saw It present.

On other days my soul was like a silkworm. It is treated with the greatest care by those who raise it. They feed it on tender leaves; having reached maturity it commences to spin with its mouth a thread of very delicate silk and makes its cocoon. It finds so much pleasure and comfort in this, it does not realize it will ever cease to exist; finally its strength being exhausted, it remains fastened up in its cocoon and dies there. I saw, or rather was shown, something similar in my soul. With the like sweetness and the same silence the soul goes on spinning silk and giving to God what she has received from Him. After the example of the little silkworm, she shuts herself within herself as in a tomb, which separates her from creatures, and with tender love, which she draws unceasingly from the depths of her heart, she longs to leave this life. Death is the true life of such a soul, and she would wish to have a thousand lives to sacrifice for God and thus merit greater favors from Him. Everything then disquiets and wearies her; nothing can satisfy her except to give her life for the Well-Beloved.

Once, at Pontoise, I complained to our Lord that I was entirely unfit for the office with which I was charged. I represented to Him my poverty, telling Him I was nothing more than a straw. And the Divine Master replied: "It is with straws I light the fire."

On another occasion, the Saturday after the Feast of the Exaltation of the Cross, while we were reciting the Hours, I felt within my soul a great desire to please God, if I could, in some way. But I realized that I was only a little worm of the earth, and neither knew nor could do anything for God or man. However, I perceived that there burned in my heart an intense desire to perform all my works in such a way as would win glory for God and my holy Mother Teresa of Jesus; I wished no other recompense for my labors. I experienced great tenderness of love, and deep recollection took possession of my soul. Jesus Christ was close to me and He said: "This is how I wish you to be, without power or knowledge, in order that I may do with you as I will; for the wise of this world with their human prudence do not listen to Me; they think they know everything."

I enjoyed the greatest consolation in this convent at Pontoise. I saw, with pleasure, that the young girls under my guidance observed with perfect fidelity the rules and constitutions. But I was not slow to notice that the Superiors had formed the design to recall me to Paris to place me at the head of the convent. This caused me great pain, because I would be in the midst of a very large city, and a city where the Court resided. One day while in a sort of interior agony, and confused at not finding myself entirely resigned to go to Paris, I became deeply recollected; and as it appeared clear to me that God wished this of me, I feared to excuse myself. Therefore, I made again the firm resolution to obey in all things the good pleasure of our Lord, and I said to him: "Do with me, Lord, as Thou wilt; I see clearly that I am not capable of this charge: even the thought fills me with great fear; besides it is a great disgrace for me to meet with honor. Why, my Lord, dost Thou wish to submit me to this trial?" At the same time my Adorable Master appeared to me in His humanity and His glory; there was so brilliant a light from the heavens where He was, even to me, that it seemed He was quite close to me; and He said to me: "It is in this way they should walk who do the works of God, for so I walked on earth, afflicted in the midst of honor and dishonor." At these words I experienced joy, consolation and inexpressible love; I was lost in astonishment and gained courage to go to Paris.

At this time, and before passing an entire year at Pontoise, enjoying, as I have already said, great consolations, and considering myself blessed in living with such holy souls, I received a new favor from the Divine Master. One day, when in the refectory, I entered for some moments into a supernatural recollection, and during this short space of time our Lord appeared to me in this manner: He was in heaven, in glory; between Him and myself there was a very great distance; it was not like other visions. He showed me that soon the Superiors would take me to Paris, that I must be prepared for this; that I would endure greater labors and contempt than I had already passed through. It was not without some sorrow that I heard this prediction; for one reason that I was weak, and another because our Lord treated me in the monastery of Pontoise as if I were in heaven; He showered favors on me; it seemed as if He was always near me for every need; He spoke to me, taught me what I must do, as a father teaches his children. I must acknowledge, also, it cost me much to separate from these souls who seemed like angels. The Divine Master did not allow them to touch the earth; He bore them, so to speak, in His arms, so great was the consolation and spiritual joy He bestowed on them. Then, too, the people of Pontoise were so good and such true Christians. Our intimacy was so great, one would have thought I had been born in their midst. No sooner did they learn in the city that it was necessary to remove me from the monastery, than the men would have taken up arms to prevent it. Therefore, it was necessary that I should leave at midnight, and oblige the religious in the name of obedience to keep the secret. One of the Superiors came to me, bringing with him one of my nephews who was studying at Paris; and to prevent my being recognized they took off my mantle and placed my nephew's cloak on my shoulders and his hat on my head. In this way we left the city, for at Pontoise the gates of the city are not closed at night. The religious did not learn of my departure until the morning, when she who replaced me went with them to chant at Mass. Then there was such a demonstration of sobbing and tears that it soon became known in the city that I had gone. All the citizens, particularly those who had daughters in the community, seeing their grief, were filled with sorrow at my departure.

CHAPTER VIII

GOVERNS CONVENT AT PARIS

The Blessed Mother Arrives at Paris From Pontoise and Governs the First
Convent as Prioress—Assistance Given Her by Isabel of the Angels—
Departure of This Sister on the Foundation of Amiens—Fervor of the
Novices at Paris—Happy Death of Angelique of the Trinity, Daughter
of the Marshal de Brissac.

On my arrival at Paris, I received the heartiest welcome from
all the novices. There was then in the convent no other professed nun but Eleanor of St. Bernard, to whom I owed much on
this occasion as well as on many others. But our novices were
very numerous; they were put under my direction, and notwithstanding my charge of Prioress, I was commanded to take care of
them. Mother Anne of Jesus and her two companions had gone
to make a foundation in Burgundy. One day while recommending
them to God, He made me understand that Mother Isabel of the
Angels was suited for France. I told M. de Berulle; and the result proved the truth of my words, for this Mother acquitted herself of her Office in a most perfect and religious manner. They
brought her from Dijon to Paris. She remained three months with
us. During the time we were permitted to be together, we both
experienced a renewal of courage and very great consolation. This
Mother was of great assistance to me in the Choir. She succeeded
in everything, because she had learned the method of leading and
appeared full of sweetness. This is required for souls in France,
because they are docile and inclined to virtue. Therefore, one
succeeds better by gentleness with them than by any other way,
and, provided it is done in a kind manner, one can make known to
them all their faults; they will take it in good part. Certainly,
for my part, I consider this method best and conformed to the
character of our Lord Jesus Christ; for if we stop to consider we
will see that He lived as a brother and a companion with His disciples. Just now many things occur to my mind to say; but I
will refrain, fearing to do it poorly and to show little humility
by entering on this subject. I have neither the capacity nor humility
requisite.

Mother Isabel of the Angels took from here for the foundation
of Amiens three professed religious, excellent subjects, and two
novices. They arrived at Amiens on the eve of Pentecost; and, the
following day, the Blessed Sacrament was placed in the Oratory of
their monastery, to the great satisfaction of the entire city, which
made a great demonstration of devotion on this occasion. The
Bishop, so they wrote, had the head of St. John the Baptist carried in procession, and celebrated a Pontifical Mass. I was much
consoled on hearing the news at Paris, and to know that all was

Life of Blessed Anne of St. Bartholomew

going on well. I must add that I was asked to be sent on this foundation, but it was not then possible.

I will speak now of our novices, who had asked me of the Superiors as their Mistress. I could not be more pleased with them, and they were also with me. I had certainly great reason to be so at the sight of such souls and the graces with which God favored them; He was lavish in their regard, but they were souls capable of great virtue. Though they were so recollected and so faithful to all the observances, I established as a rule that, before being admitted to profession, they should pass the fifteen days preceding in spiritual exercises and such perfect retirement as not to speak to anyone or see anyone. I acted thus because profession is an act which requires an exalted disposition; and I saw that our Lord had given it to them. It was in this way I caused the profession to be made by twenty-eight religious in Paris.

In order that it may be seen how advantageous it is to serve the Lord, I wish to narrate here the happy death of a Carmelite religious named Angelique, in this house at Paris, a daughter of M. de Brissac.

One night while I was sleeping, as well as I could judge, I saw in my cell, with the eyes of the spirit, a bright light; I was frightened, thinking God was calling me; I was not prepared; I had no confessor, and it was necessary I should have one at that moment. While thus troubled I learned by a supernatural light that it was Sister Angelique whom God called to Himself. He sent her a very painful malady, which caused her great suffering. She showed admirable patience and God in return gave her great consolation and special light. For until her last moment, she spoke to us with great edification, and it was consoling to hear her. She communicated several times during the short time of her illness. And a few hours before death, she received our Lord in great transports of joy. She again asked pardon of the community, as she had already done before receiving Extreme Unction. She bade farewell to all, not as one who is about to die, but as if she were departing for another monastery, saying, "Adieu!" and she added: "Give me the Blessed Virgin." She became quiet, smiling sweetly; not one of us believed she was dead, for she had given no sign to indicate it. She was a most pure soul, and it was very evident she had preserved her baptismal innocence.

CHAPTER IX

HER ZEAL FOR SOULS

Favor She Received in Paris, the Eve of the Feast of St. Denis, the Areopagite—Her Zeal for the Salvation of Souls From the Time She Commenced Mental Prayer, Above All Since She Had Lived in the Company of St. Teresa—An Occasion on Which This Zeal Increased in Her Soul at Paris.

On the eve of the Feast of St. Denis, the Areopagite, for whom I had great devotion, while in prayer, our Lord granted me the favor to visit my soul and transform it into His by a wonderful union. Though this visit lasted but a short time, its effects were very great. I became so spiritual in soul and body, that it seemed I no longer performed any natural action, or made the least natural movement. The following day, the Feast of St. Denis, our Lord granted me the same favor after Holy Communion. Although this visit was short, as I have already said, the fruits which I experienced and the dispositions in which it placed my soul, lasted more than fifteen days. Although I saw nothing, I felt within myself, in the depths of my soul, the Sovereign Majesty, as if I saw the Most Holy Trinity. I saw nothing, but the realization I had of His presence within me was more striking than if I had seen Him. During these days I had, indeed, some cause for trouble, but my mind did not allow one distracting thought to enter and lost none of its simplicity; I make use of this expression, because the vision I had of God was simple, quiet and undisturbed.

After these days had passed, it was no longer so. It is true this grace was not entirely taken from me, but it was not granted me in such perfection as I have just described. The fruit it continued to produce in me was greater courage of soul, more intense fervor, a more ardent desire to see God and to employ myself in His service according to His good pleasure. In this state there is greater activity and less of that simple looking towards God. The movements being, in all cases, more energetic, greater care is required in order not to commit faults, whereas one is preserved from them when made firm by the power of the prayer spoken of, that is to say, the simple looking towards God. The difference between these two states is easy to be understood. The soul who enjoys this simple sight of God resembles a person who is satiated and has an abundance of all the dishes possible to desire, without even the trouble of seeking them or even sitting down to the table. The soul which no longer has this simple sight of God is like a hungry man, who desires dishes according to his taste, but must procure them by labor, and if he must be solicitous in order to procure them, he must also be the same in order to preserve them. The soul must act in the same manner regarding the virtues, the knowledge of God and self: this exercise is so important, that who-

Life of Blessed Anne of St. Bartholomew

ever does not seriously enter into it will always be poor in soul. The knowledge of truth gives repose to the heart, and causes a soul to be resigned in great and little things to all God asks of her.

As soon as I commenced a life of prayer, our Lord gave me an ardent desire for the salvation of souls; this desire was greater at certain times than at others. But, since having the happiness of knowing my Holy Mother Teresa, our Lord has enkindled in me a much more intense desire for the salvation of souls, and particularly for the conversion of heretics. It was the holy Mother who communicated to me this disposition, and she rejoiced greatly when she saw this fire of zeal was consuming my soul.

However, on the occasion of the clothing of Sister Clare of the Blessed Sacrament, God increased this grace in my soul, and gave it to me in a more excellent way. The desire for the salvation of souls and the conversion of heretics was like a fire of love within me, from which arose a powerful, unconquerable flame, which, so to speak, held sway over all and drew all things to itself.

Adversity is powerless against this charity; rather it is vanquished and submissive and serves only to strengthen the spirit, as wood thrown on the fire prevents it from being extinguished; so adversity keeps this divine fire burning in the soul, and causes it to rise more rapidly towards Him who is its wished-for end. In this thirst for souls one fears neither perils nor any kind of labor: they are rather sought after, because the pain one endures in this kind of prayer causes greater suffering than labor itself.

Here I wish to give counsel to the timid, that when they find themselves in this state, they may remain faithful to God, and may not easily give way to any anxiety which would turn them from laboring for the good of souls. For if they truly compassionate their sad condition, they would give up every satisfaction in order to fly to their assistance. Truly it is cause for grief to see that those who are capable of doing good have not the desire, while ignorant women without any talent, unworthy and incapable of any good, like myself, have the courage of strong men. I say this that God may be praised, because several poor Discalced Carmelites, contrary to the wish and advice of all, in spite of the fears and forebodings with which it was sought to deter them, bravely offered themselves for all that could befall them. As far as I am concerned, I can say that I am not sorry, and since leaving Spain I have never for one moment regretted devoting myself to this labor for the love of God; on the contrary I have always felt strengthened and consoled for having undertaken this journey. Although I came alone from my convent, having poor health, and at an age when I could hope for no improvement, I found all the consolations I could have desired if I had sought for them, because God has shown Himself unceasingly to be my true Father, never leaving my soul in any need or trouble without suddenly appearing beside me to come to my aid; may He be forever blessed!

CHAPTER X

COMMENTARY

FOUNDATION OF CONVENT AT TOURS

"To-day is the Feast of St. Martin, for whom I have great devotion, because during this octave I have often received great graces from our Lord: I do not know why."—(Life of St. Teresa, by Ribera, Book IV, Chap. XIII.)

In these words St. Teresa gives us the origin of the Carmel at Tours. Her devotion for St. Martin and his predilection for her; this is, indeed, for those who study the origin of things by the torch of faith, the real cause of the foundation of this monastery.

As for the devotion of the virgin of Avila to St. Martin, nothing can be so easily explained: the mutual sympathy and resemblance of these two great souls should be the cause of and give intensity to it. Teresa, who before founding her Order had been wounded in the heart by the dart of a seraph, and who, after receiving this first wound, had seen the same seraph at different times plunge the dart into her heart, leaving her filled with seraphic love for Jesus Christ, how could she but feel attracted towards this blessed Pontiff, whose heart, like that of St. Paul, was overflowing with love for Jesus Christ? She who from the most tender age had sighed after martyrdom, how could she but love this holy Pontiff, who, although his head did not fall under the sword of the persecutor, had not, however, lost the palm of martyrdom? She, who had been consumed with the fire of apostolic zeal, how could she but feel predilection for this Bishop, one of the most apostolic who had illuminated the Church of God since the time of the Apostles? In proportion as she studied him, her devotion increased. Seeking only for the salvation of souls, and having no other end but this in the reforming of Carmel, she was as in an ecstasy when contemplating St. Martin laboring for the conquest of souls. With Hilary of Poitiers, his holy master, he planted the faith among the Gauls, and brought to Jesus Christ innumerable legions of faithful souls. It was this Pontiff, God's chosen one, to whom, after the Apostles, our Lord communicated such great grace that he merited the wonderful honor of restoring to life, through the power of the Triune God, three dead persons who had been laid in the tomb. During all his life as a Bishop, miracles sprang from his footsteps. Wherever he was, wherever he might go, he held the gifts of heaven in his hand; he distributed them as he pleased, enlightening souls, adorning them with the grace of Christ, curing bodies, delivering them from the chains of the devil and from sickness.

At the sight of Martin causing the Trinity to be adored, Christ to be known, enkindling His love in souls, extending the boun-

73

Life of Blessed Anne of St. Bartholomew

daries of the Church, giving it new peoples, Teresa, filled with joy, fell into an ecstasy. And when the life of this Apostle, consumed with love for Christ and giving itself for Him, drew to a close, Teresa was not astonished that all the heavens had been moved, and trembled with joy, seeing it about to take its flight. The soul of the seraphic virgin, identifying itself with the sentiments of the Church, exclaimed with her: "O blessed apostle of Christ, at thy passing from earth to heaven, the saints welcomed thee with songs of joy, the choirs of angels saluted thee with transport, the army of all the celestial virtues went before thee singing hymns of triumph: the Church is strengthened by thy sanctity in heaven, Bishops are glorified by this revelation from God."

It is St. Michael who finally takes him under his care, and with his angels leads him to the throne of God, and when the Holy Trinity crowns him, when Christ takes him in His arms and presses him to His heart and conducts him to His throne; when, in a word, this soul has taken possession of paradise, Teresa's soul is carried away by the triumph of the Blessed Martin; she rejoices with the angels, she is ravished with the archangels, she cries out with the choirs of Saints and with all the virgins this invitation: "Remain with us through all eternity."

The devotion of St. Teresa was enkindled by contemplating the glory with which God adorned the tomb of St. Martin. His relics brought blessing all over the world. The tomb which enclosed them was a beacon of grace for humanity; a haven of rest for all Catholicity. The Thaumaturgus, though his soul was in heaven, still lived on earth by the power of his prodigies. From all countries of the world eyes were turned towards the tomb of St. Martin, and because of him Touraine had become, as it were, the birthplace of miracles. Kings, Pontiffs, doctors, warriors, Christians of all ranks, of all classes, hastened to seek at the tomb of St. Martin the cure of their souls and bodies. Having come from all parts of the world, the pilgrims, cured in soul and body, made known everywhere the glory and power of their deliverer. There is no country where the Church is known that does not honor the name of Martin, or where this name, when called upon, does not work miracles. Thus the miraculous power of this saint radiates from his tomb to the extremities of the earth. This is what Teresa contemplated with the eye of faith, and what gave the highest impulse to her devotion for the holy Bishop of Tours.

And he, this immortal Pontiff, whom the Church calls by the sublime title, Pearl of Bishops, from the heights of heaven sees in Teresa, founding and extending her reform, the pearl of Apostolic Virgins. At the sight of the seraphic love which consumed her heart, and the admirable mission she filled in God's Church, he looked upon her with astonished delight, and was drawn to her with an attraction of predilection. The prayers Teresa addressed him with such lively faith completely won his heart. Her prayer was heard; from this time he

Foundation of Convent at Tours

stood as her intercessor before the adorable Trinity and Jesus Christ unceasingly begging them to keep in their care and bless with gifts this magnanimous and seraphic Virgin, who lived only for their glory. And this is the cause, though then unknown to Teresa, of the wonderful graces she received in the octave of the feast of the glorious St. Martin. God even chose this octave to grant Teresa the greatest favor of her life. Let us listen to her own words: "During the second year, when Prioress of the Incarnation at Avila, during the octave of St. Martin, at the moment when Father John of the Cross had just given me communion, our Lord appeared to me in the most hidden depths of my soul, gave me His right hand and said to me: 'Look at this nail; it is the mark and token that from this day you shall be My spouse; until now you have not deserved it: henceforth you shall guard My honor, seeing in Me not only your Creator, your King and your God, but above all, seeing in Me your true Spouse: from this moment My honor is yours and your honor Mine.' "

But the prayer of the holy Bishop of Tours was not limited to recommending the seraphic reformer of Carmel to God. Continuing in heaven the pastoral solicitude which on earth he felt for the people committed to his zeal, he asked of the Holy Trinity and of Jesus Christ a small band of these apostolic virgins to dwell near his tomb, and from this center to spread the sacred fire all through Touraine. A request so much for God's glory is sure to be heard. And when Teresa entered into her glory she saw at the same time all the graces she owed St. Martin and the foundation of the Carmel of Tours predestined in the designs of God.

The time for the foundation having arrived, God, who determines the glory of His Saints in proportion to what He has received from them, wished to treat His servant and His friend, St. Martin, with rare privilege and munificence. For this reason, it was His pleasure to gather together near the tomb of this dear friend, so justly called the "Pearl among Bishops," the most precious pearls of the reformed Carmel.

It was Blessed Mary of the Incarnation, the pearl and foundress of Carmel in France, and the first Carmelite after St. Teresa placed in the ranks of the Blessed, who came to lay the foundations of this monastery. As she had prepared the first convent in Paris, and arranged it for the reception of the six Carmelites from Spain, in the same manner she prepared the convent at Tours and arranged it to receive the little colony sent from Paris.

The one who, as Prioress, was to govern this monastery, was also a pearl, whose value was known to God alone. It was Anne of St. Bartholomew, the inseparable companion of St. Teresa, the one of her daughters whom the Saint perhaps loved most tenderly on earth, and in whose arms she wished to repose during that memorable ecstasy of fourteen hours which preceded for her the clear vision of God.

But Saint Teresa was not content with sending to St. Martin the élite among her daughters; she, herself, took part in the foun-

Life of Blessed Anne of St. Bartholomew

dation. Eager to show the holy Bishop that she remembered the signal graces formerly received through his intercession, she neglected nothing that this Carmel, the fruit of his prayers, should be worthy of him and worthy of her. She appeared to her dear Tours. She encouraged her and promised to assist her. In the monastery she showed herself to her in several apparitions, giving Anne of St. Bartholomew while she was journeying from Paris to her proof of maternal love. She directed her, and established with her all the observances. Owing to the frequent visits, and to the tender marks of affection of the seraphic Mother, Anne of St. Bartholomew felt as if she were still at Avila or in some other convent in Spain with the holy foundress. Soon we will hear her, herself, making a picture in words of the happiness she experienced in the Carmel of Tours.

In the year 1615, a new pearl came to shed its lustre in the Carmel of the glorious St. Martin. It was the Venerable Mother Magdalen of St. Joseph, the first French Prioress of the Carmel at Paris, whose virtues the Church later on, by solemn decree, declared heroic. For eight months this great light shone in the Carmel of Tours; she strengthened there the traditions of sanctity that Mother Anne of St. Bartholomew had established.

Still another pearl shed its soft bright light in this privileged Carmel. It was Margaret of the Blessed Sacrament, the second daughter of Blessed Mary of the Incarnation. One fact alone will make known the whole life of this virgin; her holy Mother declared that God had made known to her that her daughter Margaret would be higher than herself in the glory of heaven.

For six years Margaret of the Blessed Sacrament lived in the Carmel of Tours, the first three years as Sub-Prioress, and the last three as Prioress. It was two years after the return of Venerable Mother Magdalen of St. Joseph to Paris, that she undertook the government of the convent.

The founder of the monastery is worthy of taking rank with the heroic virgins who lived in it. He was a noble gentleman of Touraine, M. de Fonteines-Marans, one of those manly Christians, full of primitive faith, such as St. Martin formed. He had the happiness of being a relative of Blessed Mary of the Incarnation, and was an honor to this tie of relationship. He had already, repressing the revolt of nature which it had cost him, seen two of his daughters enter the Carmel at Paris, and the emotions of his paternal heart, crowned by faith, only increased the value of the sacrifice. The older of these two daughters was Magdalen of St. Joseph, whose virtues, as we have already said, have been declared heroic by the Church. His third daughter firmly determined to belong to St. Teresa, but could not, as owing to her health she could not bear the austerities of the rule. This saintly father, then, influenced and advised by his holy relative, Mme. Acarie, founded a monastery at Tours, where his daughter would have the right to live as benefactress. Happy father, to give three daughters to St. Teresa, three spouses to Jesus Christ, and who found in them three angels who prayed unceasingly for him! By this monastery which he gave to Touraine, he became one of the most generous benefactors of his country. He will have a share in all the spiritual favors there until the end of the world. How many souls will be saved century after century by the Carmelites of this monastery! He will be forever filled with astonishment at the sight of the fruitfulness of his work. And if the separation from his three daughters wounded his fatherly heart, with what unceasing joy he will be ravished, seeing the glory with which Jesus Christ has crowned them!

Everything in the birth of this monastery foreshadowed the brightest future. But, to crown its joy, the divine Master was pleased on the very day of the foundation, to change hope to certainty. He promised Blessed Mother Anne of St. Bartholomew to assist in a particular manner, until the end of time, all those who would enter this monastery, the erection of which was granted to the prayers of his friend, St. Martin of Tours. A consoling promise, which it is to the glory of God to recount here, just as Blessed Mother Anne of St. Bartholomew has left it to us in her Autobiography.

CHAPTER XI

PERSECUTIONS AND CALUMNIES

Arrival of Blessed Mother Anne of St. Bartholomew at Tours — Persecution and Calumnies of the Heretics; How She Triumphed Over Them—Renown of the Carmelites—Chosen Subjects Who Applied—Graces and Favors With Which God Crowned His Servant in the New Monastery.

I had been three years in the monastery at Paris, when a nobleman of Touraine, M. de Fonteines-Marans, asked our religious Superiors to found a convent at Tours, on condition that I should make the foundation. Therefore, the Superiors sent me with three other religious of the monastery at Paris in whom they had confidence.

In the city of Tours there was a great number of heretics and schismatics. As soon as they saw us approaching and crossing the Loire, they said: " Oh! that they might be drowned before leaving the river, and remain there forever engulfed." They soon conceived a great hatred for me. They said that I was a wicked woman, an idol of the papists. It was my good fortune that a great servant of God, most friendly to our convent, converted by this excellent means a notorious woman. She brought her one day to our church and left her afterwards in the exterior apartments of our Out-Sisters. This she did at my advice. Towards night, in order that they might not take her away by force, she took her to another house of women, where she would be secure, and encouraged her to keep her good resolutions. The heretics who were seeking her and who had seen her enter our church and the part of the house occupied by the Out-Sisters, said that we were all like her, and that we had children within the enclosure of the convent. This report was spread with so much malice, that even the Catholics became somewhat doubtful. To stop and refute this calumny, I begged one of the magistrates of the city, a man known for his integrity, and who was one of our friends, to do us the favor to enter the cloister. I told him, the monastery not being finished, I intended having some cells built, and that it would give me great pleasure if he would visit the entire convent to give me some advice regarding this matter. My intention in acting thus was to prove to him the falseness of the reports which were being spread regarding us—that I admitted men into the cloister by a secret door, which must be in the upper part of the monastery. He therefore entered; I took him everywhere and begged him to notice how all was arranged. After this visit, when he had seen all with his own eyes, he defended us in the city; he said he was convinced of our innocence, that he had visited the entire cloister, and that our having a secret door was false.

78

Persecutions and Calumnies

For my part, such calumnies did not disturb me in the least, because I knew that sooner or later the truth would be known. They had lied most frightfully, and I laughed at it all. This news was carried twenty leagues away amongst heretics who could not visit us. It even reached Paris; and one of our Superiors came post haste from that city to Tours in order to discover what could have given cause for such odious calumnies.

In the midst of this great trouble I recalled the vision I had when coming to make the foundation at Tours. The Saint appeared to me on the way, just as she was when still living. While I was walking in her company, I noticed that we were passing through thorns which did not prick us. The Saint drew near me and said: "Go forward with courage; soon I will treat you a little better." It was not long before I experienced the truth of these words. The calumnies with which they wished to stain our honor were but harmless thorns which could not wound me; and I enjoyed in this new monastery a peace and repose which quickened the life of my soul.

The heretics, however, continually pursued us with their hatred. One day a servant of one of these heretics, who was very rich, made a hole in the wall of the yard where we kept the chickens. I had it closed and made known to the gentleman that one of his servants wished to take our chickens, and that I was certain he knew nothing of it, for I considered him too honorable a man to tolerate anything of the kind. He was astonished at this message, seeing that we did not consider him a heretic; and I have since been told that he has returned to the bosom of the church. What touched him deeply, and gained his heart, was that far from making any complaint against him before the magistrates who had come for information on the subject, we said that we considered him an honorable man. This caused admiration among the seculars. They said: "These Teresians, whether we will it or will it not, will end by converting us all to the faith." Truly, I longed for it with all my heart; I treated them with great respect and honor. There were with me excellent religious who desired their conversion with the same zeal and offered unceasing prayers for this end. Notwithstanding all the attempts of calumny to lower us in public opinion, this monastery, which God protected, exhaled a marvelous odor of virtue. Wealthy young ladies belonging to the highest families came from afar to ask for the habit. One day twenty met there together asking for this favor. It was truly reason for giving praise to God.

There, under the protection of St. Martin of Tours, God granted me great favors. I had no director, it is true. I was alone, without anyone to whom I could make known the interior of my soul. He to whom I confessed did not understand one word of Spanish, and I did not understand French. The Superior of the Order only came once a year, but that did not trouble me at all. God filled me with consolation. He gave me at Tours the favors of which He had deprived me at another time. He granted

Life of Blessed Anne of St. Bartholomew

me some which kept me for several days strong in His spirit and by the aid of which I could practice, with great facility, exercises of penance and virtue. Crosses, it seemed to me, had doubled my strength. Without knowing how, I kept recollected in the presence of God. I acknowledge that God then gave me experience of the spirit of St. Paul; and I felt that He made me understand it was the same God who inspired St. Paul who gave me this spirit, so that it was by experimental knowledge that I could say: "Who now will separate us from the charity of Jesus Christ?" No, nothing, neither labors nor the want of necessary things. I was really intoxicated with love; and if this God who had given it to me had not at the same time given me strength, Nature, left to herself, could not have borne it. In this state, I said also like St. Paul: "I desire to be anathema and to die for my brethren and for Jesus Christ my Savior."

As on such occasions the soul offers herself with love and an entire, unconditional resignation, without reserve, this Adorable Master said to me in this very Monastery of Tours: "The glory of the just is to do My will." But these words, that the glory of the just consisted in doing His will, He said to me with ineffable love; my soul was so deeply touched, I was as if exalted and carried out of myself.

CHAPTER XII

VISIONS

Efficaciousness of Her Prayers for Elenor of Bourbon, Aunt of King Henry IV, Abbess of Frontevrault—Edifying Death of This Princess—Prophetic Light of Blessed Mother Anne of St. Bartholomew—Apparition of Father Jerome Gratien of the Mother of God and of Dona Casilda de Padilla, Daughter of the Adelantando of Castille—Our Lord's Consoling Promise to the Carmelites of the Monastery at Tours.

While I was at Tours, the Abbess of Frontevrault, whose place is only about two days' journey from the city, fell ill. Her nieces, the Princesses of Longueville, were with her. The elder one, who was acquainted with me, wrote to me frequently to give news of the state of her aunt's health. I desired to serve them as far as was in my power. I owed it to them, as without my having in any way merited it, they were very kind to me and had consoled me in my troubles. I, therefore, recommended the Abbess to God, praying that this God of goodness would grant her the graces to make her salvation certain; to speak truly, I was not without anxiety for her; she had to give account of several monasteries under her Abbey, which, owing to a succession of wars and heresies, had become lax and were going to destruction. Therefore, I repeat, I feared for her. One day, the sick nun and her nieces sent me word to pray for her with all the fervor I could; in fact, death was approaching and God allowed me to know it. The physician who attended her was very faithful in coming to give me an account of her condition. That day when he came to the monastery, God had already shown me that the sick nun was in extremity and that she was in need of my prayers. Becoming immediately recollected in prayer, I saw a legion of demons entering the apartment of the Abbess. Her poor soul was plunged in deep affliction. At this sight I was filled with grief, but at the same time I felt great confidence in God. In my affliction I turned towards God, with the hope that He would grant me the favor I asked, and immediately I saw Jesus Christ as He was when He conversed in this world, vested as a Bishop and divinely beautiful, enter the apartment of the dying nun. He was wonderfully majestic; and was accompanied by a great number of angels and saints. Suddenly, as if overwhelmed by His appearance, all the wicked spirits fled, rushing out through the first means of escape. At the same time I saw this blessed soul come out of her agony, and the Divine Master took her with him. They said that she had been very good; in all that depended on her she had proved herself an excellent religious, and was very charitable towards her religious in their troubles.

This apparition of the Abbess of Frontevrault was not the only one. I received others of persons still living and far distant from me.

81

Life of Blessed Anne of St. Bartholomew

Father Jerome Gratien of the Mother of God appeared to me two or three times during his life, while he was oppressed by suffering and afflictions. He allowed me to see what he was enduring. He appeared to me since, when the Turks wished to make him a martyr in Africa. He showed me the fire they had prepared and in which they wished to burn him. But I did not see the other torments to which they subjected him. I saw only the fire which was kindled and into which they intended casting him. I then saw some Moorish women who craved pardon for him. I saw that the Father was not thrown into the fire, and that he felt inexpressible grief because the palm of martyrdom was not for him.

And now another vision of this kind was granted me.

A religious, Casilda de Padilla, after having made her profession in our house at Valladolid, was obliged to leave this monastery. Her parents, with the authority of an order they had obtained from the Pope, obliged her to enter another Order. She was under the impression that this Order, which was that of St. Francis, aspired to greater austerities than the one she had left. Therefore, she thought she would find greater consolation there and less affection would be shown her, for the marks of esteem shown her caused her great suffering; she was the daughter of the adelantando of Castille. This blessed spouse of Jesus Christ merited by her character and virtue these marks of esteem; and as she was truly humble no one could help loving her. While our own Saint was in this convent at Valladolid, Casilda went to visit her, for the Saint had great regard for her, but when she could not speak to our Mother she came to me and remained with me a night and day. For the friendship we felt for each other was very great. When Casilda left this monastery, we were no longer there. She appeared to me at Avila, being still alive. She was deeply afflicted and said to me: "Oh! my Sister, what pain I suffer where they have placed me!" This caused me great grief because I loved her very much. She had asked to go to the monastery at Avila in order to be far from her parents, but could not obtain permission. When she appeared to me, as I have said, I was fully thirty leagues distant from her.

Sunday after the Ascension, the day on which the Most Blessed Sacrament was placed with great solemnity in this house of Tours, while I was preparing for communion and asking our Lord. that this beginning might receive His blessing, and that with this same blessing He would deign to assist all of us who were present and all who would enter until the end, this Adorable Master gave me great assurance that He would do so, and that He granted my request. From that moment until the present day, I have known by experience that this favor has been granted us, both by its visible effects and its work in the souls of our Sisters.

FOURTH BOOK

CHAPTER I

DEPARTURE FROM PARIS

Departure From Paris 5th of October, 1611—Arrival at the Carmel of St. Joseph of Mons—Sojourn for One Year in This Monastery.

I left Paris the day following the anniversary of the death of the Saint. Although I had no desire to go to Flanders, I took this journey, my soul filled with the consolations which God sent me. I remembered that when leaving Spain, I had a vision which seemed to me of little importance. I saw that I would not remain seven entire years in France, and that before the expiration of this time, I should go to the Netherlands. And so it was: five or six days were wanting to the termination of the seven years.

Before leaving Tours our Lord showed me a light, and by the aid of this light I saw a house; it was precisely the one that served as a dwelling when we took possession of our new foundation at Antwerp. I recognized it, as well as the young lady whom our Lord also showed me in this vision. She was the first received and was called Teresa of Jesus.

When I arrived at Mons I was very cordially welcomed by our Sisters. I remained in their midst just one year.

CHAPTER II

FOUNDATION AT ANTWERP

Anne of Saint Bartholomew Appointed to Make the Foundation at Antwerp —Revelation Regarding the Great Destiny of This Monastery—It Was Founded on the 6th of November, 1612—Assistance From the Jesuits at Antwerp—Choice Subjects Who Made Application—Mlle. de Dompré Was the First to Take the Habit and Received the Name of Teresa of Jesus—The Best Site in the City Was Chosen for the Building of the Convent—Assistance of Our Lord and of St. Teresa.

During my stay in the Monastery of St. Joseph at Mons, they spoke of the foundation at Antwerp. I did not in the least anticipate such a mission; I was certain they would give the charge to one more capable than I. I was obliged to accept it since obedience imposed it on me. The day following that on which the will of the Superiors had been made known to me, whilst recollected after communion, I turned towards our Lord, and recommended this project most earnestly to Him; I begged Him to give me grace to act in all things according to His good pleasure, and to inspire my Superiors not to give me charge of this undertaking, in case He did not wish it. This Adorable Master consoled me, as He had done on other occasions, and said to me: "Take courage, and believe that this foundation will give light to all this country." After these words I took courage to embrace the cross, and did not doubt that our Lord's promise would be fulfilled.

From the beginning of this foundation, God brought us very capable souls, with great interior spirit, subjects who were accomplished and belonged to the ranks of the nobility, and this to the great astonishment of all worldly people. I maintain for a certainty that the Saint governed this house and took especial care of it, and that our Lord did the same, as has been known by experience on several occasions.

On our arrival in this city our poverty was so great that we had only fifty florins, and even this was borrowed. The Fathers of the Society of Jesus gave us all that was necessary to celebrate the first Mass, for we had absolutely nothing. The magistrates from the beginning were not favorable to us, and wished to send us back; but God had arranged everything in such a way that this monastery was esteemed by the entire city. During the three years we have been here, in all that regards the Church it has been better provided than others in ten years. We have bought the best site in the whole city. I had neither solicitude nor grief; God gave me such lively faith, such a conviction that it was our Lord Himself who took care of the convent and the Saint was the Prioress, that very often I imagined I was still serving her as I had done when she was living, and that she did the rest. I often had proof of this.

84

Foundation at Antwerp

It was not imagination, it was the truth; and now even while writing these pages I have felt that she was with me, and that it is she who directs all and governs in my place. God has by this means given me a peace, a consolation which surpasses all that one can imagine. My prayer has been more continual and God has given me in it greater favors.

CHAPTER III

WONDERFUL FAVORS FROM GOD

Zeal With Which She Burned for the Glory of God, for the Church, and the Salvation of Souls—This Zeal Becomes a Real Martyrdom—Light Received on Holy Thursday Regarding the Passion of Jesus Christ—Eternal Salvation is the Fruit of This Meditation—Vision at the Profession of a Religious and at the Renewal of Vows by the Community—Vision on the Feast of the Immaculate Conception and on the Feast of the Three Kings—Wonderful Favors She Received From the Divine Master.

Since my arrival at Antwerp our Lord has in a very noticeable manner diffused into my soul the unction of His love and His charity. I have almost continually enjoyed the presence of God. From time to time I have shown more tenderness of charity, I have had a more ardent desire for the spiritual welfare of my neighbor; at other times I have felt an ardent thirst for the salvation of souls and an insatiable zeal for the exaltation of the church. This charity, I can say in all truth, causes me a real martyrdom of heart, and I cannot resist it.

At the sight of the needs of the Church, my soul experiences great intensity of zeal. When I seek pardon for sinners and to appease His anger, God shows me such great love that I know not how to express the feelings of my soul, it is as if my soul, free from the dominion of the flesh, sees herself in a place of sweetness and delights, where she finds in her one Well-Beloved and Master all that she can desire. Truly she desires nothing for herself; her only desire is for the honor and glory of her Well-Beloved. This is why she repeats to Him unceasingly: "Lord make Thyself known to all, so that all may love Thee; do not permit, my tender Master, that souls should be ignorant of who Thou art." The soul utters these words with great love and great confidence, and she adds: "I know, my Lord, if Thou wilt reveal Thyself and wilt try to make Thyself known, all will love Thee." And this Divine Master is so pleased that I should speak to Him in this manner, that He shows ever-increasing love for me. O Infinite Goodness! what confusion for me when this vision has passed away, to realize that this infinitely good God does look at my faults, but seeks only to make Himself known to me in order that I may love Him. He who is Love itself! At first it is by a tiny light and a little sweetness that He appeals to the soul, but this light and this sweetness are like a small fire which is kindled at first by straw and, if afterwards wood is thrown on it, becomes a great fire whose heat is unendurable.

One Holy Thursday our Lord showed me the immense love of the mystery of the day, and the great love this Adorable Master bears towards souls. Whilst my soul was delighting in these divine mysteries, our Lord gave me to understand, that if each

Wonderful Favors from God

day we would think once only of His Sacred Passion and of the love with which He suffered for us, no matter how short this consideration might be, it would suffice for our salvation and draw great graces upon us. The love of God which I experienced in contemplating this mystery was so great, it seemed as if my soul was about to separate from my body, and that my last hour had come. If God had not put an end to this transport, it would have been impossible for me to bear it. As a consequence of this favor my soul was so peaceful and so filled with the love of God, that I would have been glad to have taken all my Sisters and all creatures into my heart. From that time I felt, in all the powers of my soul, greater strength than formerly.

On another occasion, while a religious was making her profession, I was seized with an ecstasy of love of God, and my soul entered into deep recollection. When she was pronouncing her vows, I saw that the Infant Jesus received them and, carrying them away with Him, presented them to the Eternal Father.

Another time two religious were making their profession in this monastery, and I saw that our Holy Mother was between them, having a very majestic appearance, which was given her by God.

At Paris while two religious were making their profession, I also saw our Holy Mother and our Lord Jesus Christ, between them.

Here at Antwerp the Divine Master was pleased to favor me with another vision. On the Feast of the Presentation of the Blessed Virgin, being all assembled in Chapter, we renewed our vows after the example of our Holy Mother, who left us this custom and wished this renewal should be made on the very day when the Virgin was presented in the Temple. After having pronounced our vows at Chapter, we went to the Choir to present them to the Most Blessed Sacrament. My soul entering there into recollection, our Lord did me the favor to show me how agreeable this act had been to Him, and that the Sisters would continue in His grace in recompense for the act they had made with their whole heart.

At certain times our Lord deigns to show my soul greater familiarity than usual. He gives me then unbounded confidence that He will be pleased with all that I ask of Him. Here is an account of what happened to me in this house at Antwerp. On the eve of the Feast of St. Catherine, a letter was brought to me in which I was shown how insignificant I was, and my incapacity for governing. I remained calm, without yielding to the least unfavorable thought. I went to the Choir and said to the Divine Master that I wished only to live for Him and His honor. He appeared to me as He was on this earth, with a countenance radiating peace and great majesty. He remained for some time at my side, then disappeared. So great a favor caused my soul to enter into profound recollection, and the impression it made upon me remained several days.

Life of Blessed Anne of St. Bartholomew

On the Feast of the Immaculate Conception and the Octave day, I had wonderful consciousness of the presence of the Blessed Virgin and of this mystery. One day during the Octave in particular, I had an intellectual vision of the Blessed Virgin all resplendent in glory; but this vision lasted only a short time.

One day I felt greatly mortified because my age and weakness would not permit me to perform as much penance as I wished. Our Lord made me understand that the most important thing does not consist in performing wonderful exterior acts and showing great feeling, but a good heart is what He prizes and wishes from us. This, it is to be understood, is when we cannot do the good that we desire.

During the Octave of the Feast of the Three Kings, while recollected in prayer, I meditated on this mystery for which God had given me particular devotion. I saw the most Holy Virgin with the Infant Jesus in her arms, and she made me understand that He very often dwelt in my heart in the same way.

My Adorable Master quite often taught me how I should govern, and this was a very great grace for me, as I was so ignorant and simple.

He deigned quite often also to grant me the highest favors, without my having merited them, and without my knowing how to make Him any return.

On the Feasts of All Saints and All Souls, I have always received particular graces from this Adorable Savior; but this past year, during the entire Octave, He was pleased to shower His graces upon me, showing me at the same time greater love. One could not believe with what love He treats this poor soul, so ungrateful and so faithless. Sometimes I feel our Lord as intimately united to my soul as if He were my Brother. One day during this Octave, I was awakened by Him, and when I awoke my whole soul was so inflamed with love I could not bear it, and yet this Adorable Master united Himself more and more closely to my soul; at last He opened His Heart and placed me therein.

There my soul enjoyed something of this wonderful ecstasy; in truth, the transport did not seem to me to have lost any of its intensity, but it was sweeter; as a fire, which, without raging, gently burns itself out. This love does not always act in this manner in the soul, but comes and goes. As for feeling Jesus Christ united to my soul, the truth is, that though I do not see Him, I have greater certainty, it seems to me, that I possess Him than if I saw Him. During the time I enjoyed this precious companionship, I felt not the slightest effort in the practise of virtue; my soul was raised to such a state of simplicity that, in the practise of virtue, what was painful to it before, now became easy. The only difficulty is regarding the soul; it is as if water were flowing over a stone without making an impression.

APPENDIX

CHRONICLES OF ANTWERP

To the Account of the Blessed Mother, Taken from the Manuscript Chronicle of the Convent of Antwerp.

From the time of her arrival at Antwerp, the 29th of October, the year 1612, our holy Mother experienced the first effects of that loving Providence which had been her support, in the fortress where she was lodged with her companions, in the home of Don Ignatius Borgia, who was governor at the time. He lived there with Madame Helena, his wife. They both considered themselves very happy to receive one whom they honored as a Saint, and who was revered as such by everyone. This Blessed Mother received from these persons proofs of unusual kindness, which have become like an inheritance in their noble families. And this kind interest has ever continued toward the mother and her daughters, who in gratitude desire to render immortal the memory of their generous benefactors.

God also, who took care of all that concerned His faithful servant, wished to carry out her desire in this matter, rewarding a hundredfold the favors she and her daughters received from this nobleman. Don Ignatius, carried away by the passion for gambling, was in danger of being lost; he owed the origin and progress of his conversion, as he himself has declared, to our Mother, and this grace was the reward of the hospitality he had shown them. He chose her from that time as his advocate with God, and as his spiritual Mother. Under her holy direction he changed his life entirely, and wept over his sins with the greatest sorrow. Every day, notwithstanding his occupations and cares, he went to consult her, or at least ask her blessing. She was so prudent in the spiritual guidance of this nobleman, in causing him to give up all his bad habits, stripping himself of the old Adam to clothe himself anew with Jesus Christ, that he persevered constantly in the path of salvation which she had pointed out to him, and merited by his penance and contrition for his sins to die the death of the just.

The Reverend Fathers of the Society of Jesus, always apostolic men, gave ample proof of it, by helping with their discourses and their altar furnishings these poor servants of Jesus Christ. It was they who heard their confessions until the year 1618.

Our Blessed Mother had a white wax candle burned during all the Divine Office in the choir of the church, in honor of our holy Mother St. Teresa, in order that she might be pleased to take interest in assisting her daughters; which custom has been observed since and is continued even at present. Therefore, they have never been in want of the necessaries of life. But here is another admirable proof of the divine Providence which brought

Life of Blessed Anne of St. Bartholomew

them help and assisted them in their sickness and infirmities. During the first days that they were in this little house, Reverend Mother Mary of the Holy Spirit was taken so ill one night that our Blessed Mother feared losing her; and, as they did not yet know any physician, they did not call one. But our Saint, according to her custom, only made known her need to our Lord; then going to the front door, which she opened at four o'clock in the morning, and calling the only person who was in the street, she addressed these words to him: "Are you not a physician?" He replied, "Yes," and she took him in to see her sick one. Then it was learned that this was M. Nugnez, first physician in the city, who from that time until his death continued charitably to attend and assist with much affection the sick of the house and considered himself well recompensed for his trouble, in having had the happiness of being a witness of the holy death of the Blessed Foundress of our Monastery.

Our Mothers lived almost three years in this House; where the perfume of their sanctity and above all that of their holy Superior rejoiced all hearts, and won for them a greater amount of esteem and affection than all the contradictions and opposition they had suffered in their holy undertaking. They began to receive such generous alms that they shared it with others, and continued to live thus very comfortably as far as our rule will allow, without having bank account or revenue, until the year 1636. The Blessed Mother then thought the time had come to dig the foundations for the new building in which they were to live. It was necessary to choose the site. Having visited several places with Father Thomas of Jesus, then Superior of that province, without being satisfied, she stopped finally before the spot where the monastery now stands, on a street commonly called the Rose-tree, and near the great parade ground which is between the city and the citadel. Immediately on discovering this spot, so far from human traffic and so near the fields and the country, she said to Father Thomas of Jesus: "This is the place, my Father, where the songs of the birds will draw our minds to recollection."

They then purchased this property, which had on it several small houses, with a garden large enough to build a poor cloister; and without delay our Blessed Mother went to live there with all her daughters. Divine Providence was no less favorable on this occasion than heretofore; for at this time He inspired Mlle. de Vertain, maid of honor to the Infanta Isabella and daughter of Count de Vertain, to ask for the habit of a poor Carmelite, under the direction of our Blessed Mother whose sanctity was in so great renown throughout the whole court. As soon as she had obtained the favor she asked, their Serene Highnesses, the Archduke Albert and the Infanta Isabella, with whom it was customary to honor their maids of honor with parental kindness, deigned to make a journey to this city, expressly for the purpose of assisting at the clothing of this one, which took place during the first part of September of the year 1615. And, to give greater proof of their piety and of their devotion toward our Blessed Mother and our holy Order which she was endeavoring to establish, they wished at the same time to lay the first stone in her convent; under this stone they placed two silver medals which were found some time after, when in order to give a better form to the building they were obliged to destroy what had been commenced. The larger of these medals bears a Latin inscription, the translation of which we give:

"Albert and Isabella, by the grace of God, Infantas of Spain, Archdukes of Austria, Dukes of Burgundy and Brabant, Counts of Flanders and Holland, with their own hands these pious and happy princes have placed the first stone of this church in the year 1615."

On the reverse of the same medal there is engraven a front view of the church, and this inscription: "Dedicated to the Blessed Teresa, Mother of the Carmelites."

On the other medal, which is smaller, on one side is the picture of the Archduke Albert, and on the reverse, that of the Infanta Isabella.

These two medals are kept as a perpetual memorial in the archives of the convent. We learn from the first, not only the year when the first stone of our monastery was laid, but also that it was dedicated to our holy Mother St. Teresa, who is called simply blessed, because she was only beatified the preceding year. We must remark, however, that it is stated in the Acts of the Monastery that it is dedicated at the same time to our glorious Patriarch St. Joseph, and to our holy Mother Teresa.

After their Serene Highnesses had thus honored the first steps of this foundation, it was very easy to obtain from the magistrates official letters of admission. Therefore they bear the date of the 26th of the same month of September, and their excellencies dispatched theirs the following day, the 27th of September of the same year, 1615.

CHAPTER IV

COMMENTARY

THE GIFT OF MIRACLES GRANTED HER

The Gift of Miracles Granted to Blessed Mother Anne of St. Bartholomew.

For the past sixty years Anne of St. Bartholomew had labored for the glory of God. Spain and France had each in their turn been the theater of her zeal. During this long space of time she had won for herself the title of most faithful and unconquerable in the service of God. In return God had glorified her in Spain and France by making her sanctity shine forth in the world; but in the Netherlands He wished in some manner to glorify her before the whole Church. He wished to show in open day how dear this seraphic virgin was to Him, and what immense credit she enjoyed with Him. He made His greatness shine forth in her; He treated her as a true Spouse, placed in her hands the treasures of His grace and His clemency. He adorned her in an incomprehensibly higher degree than before, with the gift of miracles and prophecy. He made her name illustrious throughout the whole world and finally, by the graces with which He unceasingly enriched her, caused her to rise with the flight of an eagle to the most sublime heights of sanctity.

We will give the account of historians regarding the gift of miracles, the gift of prophecy and the renown for sanctity which made this virgin illustrious; as for the high favors which crowned the last years of her life, she herself will picture them for us.

First, regarding the gift of miracles, here is a marvel which shone forth in her during all the time of her stay at Antwerp. The inhabitants of this city having heard of the great things God had done by means of His servant in Spain and France, from the time of her arrival considered her a saint whose prayers were all powerful. Therefore they hastened to her in sickness and physical ills. They begged her to ask a cure from God, and were confident if she prayed their request would be granted. Besieged by so many entreaties, a struggle arose in her soul between her humility and her charity. She was overwhelmed at the very thought that they could believe she was capable of obtaining anything by her prayers, and on the other hand her tender compassion for those who implored her help would not allow her to abandon them. What means did she employ then to reconcile the interests of these two virtues, humility and charity? Here is the way: she blessed water, dipping in it relics of Saints that she had, in order that the effect of this water would not be attributed to her, but to the intercession of the Saints and the power of their relics. The interests of heaven and earth were in this way reconciled. The servant of God no longer restrained the

The Gift of Miracles Granted Her

ardor of her charity, and showed the compassion of the most tender of Mothers to all those who had recourse to her.

The water rendered holy by her blessings and the relics of the Saint was sent to the sick; and they no sooner drank it than they were cured, to the great astonishment of all who witnessed it. And when they went to thank her, she would say humbly that the cure was not due to her prayers, but solely to the relics of the Saints, which relics had given this virtue to the water. Her miracles were so continual and so numerous, that they might be considered as an unending miracle. After the death of the Blessed Mother they were examined, and the Bishop of Antwerp, after having scrutinized and weighed the depositions of the religious, after weighty deliberation, with the advice of theologians and physicians, confirmed and approved them. We will now recount the testimony of some of the religious on this subject.

Mother Mary of the Holy Spirit, who had filled the Office of Prioress in the Convent of Antwerp, expresses herself thus: "Blessed Mother Anne of St. Bartholomew cured several fevers in this place with water which she blessed, making three times the sign of the cross and saying three Ave Marias. To shield her humility and hide the miracle, she dipped relics of the Saints in this water."

Mother Catherine of Christ relates as follows what she witnessed while holding the office of turn-Sister in the convent at Antwerp: "While I was turn-Sister, great numbers of persons came to recommend themselves to the prayers of our blessed Mother, saying that they begged the holy Mother to recommend them to God. Not knowing at first whether by this name of holy Mother they meant our holy Mother Teresa or our saintly Prioress, I inquired and learned for a certainty that by this title they referred to Mother Anne of St. Bartholomew. Such was the renown of her sanctity and so great the faith and confidence they had in her prayers, that they came from all parts seeking the water she had blessed for the sick; and the sick who recovered their health were very numerous. Every day so many persons came to the convent, that they gave no little occupation to the turn-Sisters, and our Blessed Mother was pleased to do them a charity."

The other witnesses of so many miracles all speak in the same way.

After this general exposition of the miracles of the Servant of God, we will recount some of special interest.

As a secret of His love for His faithful servant, our Lord sent her a trial, apparently a most terrible one, in permitting one of her daughters, Anne of St. Teresa, to be struck by the pest. At this blow the affliction of the religious was unbounded. However, it far from equalled that of their saintly Mother. It was as a sword piercing her heart, when she realized the necessity of isolating the sick one from the community, and that she could neither visit her, speak with her, care for or serve her, as she was accustomed to do with the other sick, although Prioress. But this crush-

93

Life of Blessed Anne of St. Bartholomew

ing trial of the pest, after having spread fear and sorrow, was only to serve for the glory of God; it was to cause the charity and faith of the holy Prioress to shine forth in clear light; it was to exemplify the power of the Almighty in the sick one, together with the virtue of submission and the influence of Blessed Mother Anne of St. Bartholomew with God. Among the numbers who gave solemn testimony to the fact, let us listen to the testimony of the one who was miraculously cured.

"When our Lord was pleased to strike me with the plague, I was in a short time in danger, and on the point of breathing my last sigh. My whole body was cold and bathed in the death-sweat; at the same time I experienced such pain in the heart, it seemed to me every moment would be my last. During this night, great things were taking place within me; I was perfectly resigned to die. The Sister who was taking care of me came to see me; she found me in the throes of so great agony that she was greatly frightened and, leaving me, hastened to tell our holy Mother that I was on the point of giving up my soul. On hearing this our Blessed Mother charged two of the religious to tell me from her that she forbade me to die. At the same moment I felt that she was holding the hands of God, and that this great God would not carry out His designs on me, because of the fervent prayer addressed to Him by His servant. All the anguish and all the sorrow vanished; I remained in great peace of soul and filled with admiration at the sight of the great power our holy Mother had with God."

We will cite some other examples which will show that it was particularly in favor of her daughters that Blessed Mother Anne of St. Bartholomew loved to make use of her influence with God. Anne of the Presentation, while still in the world, was afflicted with severe and continual pain in the head. After receiving the habit of Carmel in the Monastery of Antwerp, she felt during the novitiate somewhat relieved. But after her profession, not only did the pains return, but they became so excessive they did not leave her a moment's repose. One day she went in desolation to find the holy Mother. Filled with compassion she made the sign of the cross on her forehead and immediately her pains ceased, never to return.

Another of her daughters was tried for six weeks by such continual and violent toothache, that she could neither eat, sleep nor take a moment's repose. She went to the Blessed Mother and begged her blessing; as soon as she had received it, she was entirely cured.

Here is an account of the manner in which the holy Prioress miraculously restored health to another of her daughters, Mary of St. Joseph. We will borrow the very words of the deposition made under oath by this religious:

"When the Sisters were sick," said Mary of St. Joseph, "she recommended them to God with so much affection that she would pass whole nights without sleeping. Once when I was suffering

The Gift of Miracles Granted Her

from fever she came to see me early in the morning and said to me: 'My daughter, I have recommended you to God and your fever will not return.' And so it was; the Divine Master cured me by her prayers."

This charity, which was so maternally tender and heavenly, could not be kept entirely within the monastery; it passed without, bringing life and health to strangers who implored her help. We can only give some examples—a large volume would be necessary to recount all.

John de Cors, an inhabitant of Antwerp, after having been long afflicted with malignant fever and ague, reached his end. Forsaken by the physicians and already in his agony, he remembered the great holiness of Blessed Mother Anne of St. Bartholomew, and at the same time felt within himself the firm conviction that through her intercession he would recover his health. He, therefore, sent some one to beg her please to recommend him to God. The Saint did not delay in assisting him; she blessed a little water and sent it to him. Scarcely did the sick person drink it than he revived, recovered his strength, and was completely cured, and, as a greater evidence of the miracle, rose from his bed and went to work in his office as if he had never been sick. This miracle gained great notoriety throughout the whole town of Antwerp.

Doctor Diego de Barreda, Chaplain of the Oratory of her Serene Highness the Infanta, and General Almoner of His Majesty's Army in the Netherlands, being at the point of death and at a great distance from the Blessed Mother, recovered his health through her intercession. While he was at death's door, the holy Prioress saw him in spirit, and, knowing his danger, recommended him to God, and obtained his restoration to life. She declared this to him herself some time after, when he visited her at the convent at Antwerp.

In the cure which we are about to relate, the Divine Master made manifest in His servant a participation in that virtue which went forth from Him, while He was on this earth, and cured all the sick.

In the Monastery of Trésiguen there lived a religious a prey to sufferings which death alone could relieve. For three years a cancer devoured and wasted her away, causing at the same time the most cruel torments. When there was no longer any remedy for her under heaven, except patience, she firmly hoped for relief in the prayers of Blessed Mother Anne of St. Bartholomew. She, therefore, came to visit her at Antwerp. Full of faith in her power with God, she begged her to lay her hand on her chest and to give her her blessing. The humble virgin at first made some excuse, but, soon overcome by the sick one and the religious who had accompanied her, she spent nine days in prayer, every day giving her blessing to the sick one. At the end of these nine days the religious was completely cured, and the miracle had the

Life of Blessed Anne of St. Bartholomew

greater weight as the gravity of the illness and the impossibility of a remedy was better known.

It was not only from her hands that this miraculous virtue went forth; but also from her clothing, as well as rosaries, pictures and papers which had been sanctified by the touch of her hands. This is what we read in the deposition of Mother Teresa of Jesus, who succeeded the servant of God in the charge of Prioress. Here are her words: "Several sick persons were cured by only wearing some object which our holy Mother had used." And Mother Mary Margaret of the Angels expressed herself thus: "A very great number of sick persons were cured by applying to their bodies papers on which she had written; others carried them about them as relics. A soldier who wore on his breast one of these papers with the handwriting of our holy Mother was miraculously delivered from death; a musket having been discharged at him, the ball pierced the clothing which covered his chest, but was stopped by the letters traced by the hand of the Saint."

CHAPTER V

COMMENTARY

SPIRIT OF PROPHECY

The gift of prophecy shone forth no less brilliantly in her than the gift of miracles.

Prophecy is a supernatural light which illuminates not only the past and the future, but also in the present, what could not be known by the natural light of reason.

Visions, revelations, apparitions, belong to the spirit of prophecy. It is proved by the account of the Venerable Mother that she was gifted with this spirit from the first years of her life until the very end of her long career.

Here we will limit ourselves to the recital of particular prophetic lights which it pleased God to grant her. It will be sufficient to show us how the prophecy of Joel, "I will give my spirit to all flesh, and your sons and daughters shall prophesy," was accomplished in her.

At Tours she saw the Abbess of Frontevrault, Eleonore de Bourbon, aunt of Henry IV, assisted at her death by our Lord.

In this same city, Casilda de Padilla, daughter of the Adelantando of Castille, of whom St. Teresa has left such an admirable portrait in the Book of Foundations, appeared to her, manifesting her soul to her and confiding to her her sorrows.

There again she saw Father Gratien, captive of the Moors in Africa, treated inhumanly by them, on the point of being cast, through hatred of the faith, into a pit; and finally delivered by the pleading of some Moorish women. Finally it was at Tours that she was once more instructed by a light which she had had in Spain; she knew that after seven years' sojourn she would leave France and go to the Netherlands. She saw the house where she would found a monastery at Antwerp, and Mlle. de Dompré, the first novice she would receive there.

At Mons she learned from our Lord's own mouth, that the foundation at Antwerp would be a torch, which would cast its splendor and light throughout the whole country.

When she was passing Marimont—villa of the Archduke Albert and the Infanta Clara-Isabella-Eugenia—noticing a young girl among the courtiers, she looked at her intently. The Infanta asking her the cause, she replied: "I look at her because she should be a religious." This reply astonished the princess, and the young girl still more, who was far from thinking then of the religious state. Therefore, she was unable to keep from shedding tears and saying: "Why should I be a religious, if I do not wish it?" "Do not weep, madamoiselle," replied the Blessed

Life of Blessed Anne of St. Bartholomew

Mother. "When you come to ask to be received, you will desire it with your whole heart." In vain she wished to resist; the prophetic words she had heard were ever present to her. Finally she yielded to the call of grace. The Infanta wrote to the Blessed Mother, that from the time she had heard her words, she knew they would be fulfilled. She received the holy habit from the hands of the Foundress of the Carmel at Antwerp, and bore in religion the name of Clara of the Cross.

John Gomez Cano had two daughters who had no thought of entering the religious life, and who, according to all appearances, were to remain in the world. However, our Lord gave His servant to understand that He had chosen them for Carmel. Following the interior movement of the Holy Spirit, she prophesied to these two young ladies their entrance at Carmel. At first they found it very difficult to believe; but when the moment of grace came, they asked most earnestly of the Blessed Mother to give them the holy habit. One received the name of Mary Teresa of Jesus, and the other that of Catherine of the Mother of God.

She propesied to Mary of St. Joseph, long before the event took place, that she would enter Carmel, and that she would be present at her death: a twofold prediction which was fulfilled.

Dona Leonora de Pastrana came one day to visit the servant of God, and brought with her her daughter, who was not fifteen months old. The Blessed Mother looked at her, and taking her lovingly in her arms, said, that God would make her a Saint. Wonderful to relate! God loosened the tongue of the little girl, and she who had not until that time uttered a word and did not talk until some months later, replied distinctly in an intelligible voice: "Amen! Amen! Amen!" Our Lord confirming the truth and certainty of the prophecy by this miracle.

Erneste de Ligne, wife of Count John de Nassau, was much grieved because she had no children. Trusting in the Blessed Mother's power with God, she went to her and begged her to obtain for her a son. Instructed by a supernatural light, the Saint replied: "Have confidence in our Lord, He will give you one." As the Saint had predicted, Erneste de Ligne gave birth to a son, but, alas! she soon saw she was in danger of losing him. Addressing herself with faith to the one who had obtained him for her, she begged her to save him by her prayers. The servant of God prayed, and the child was miraculously cured.

The following is a word for word extract from her own "Account of Her Life":

"One day during the Octave of Corpus Christi, our Lord, whilst showing me great love, invited me to make some request. The vision of the Divine Master caused me to enter into a state of supernatural recollection. I saw before me three persons: one was my sister, the other my first cousin, and the third Antonio Perey, secretary to Philip II, and all three were then far from me. I asked for the salvation of these three souls, and our Lord showed me that He granted my request. Shortly after this I

98

received letters announcing to me the death of my sister and my cousin. My sister was drowned, and my cousin had succumbed to a fever, but God had called them both the very day they appeared to me. The death of Antonio Perey proved to me also that my request had been granted. Secretary and favorite of Philip II, he had committed some misdeeds. The sentence of death had already been pronounced against him, when he managed to escape. He took refuge in England; his sojourn there was the source of still greater evils for his soul. While I was in France he came to visit me; he seemed to despair of his salvation—a feeling caused by the evil things he had done. Whilst speaking to him I felt drawn to him, and felt an ardent desire for his salvation. I have since been told our Lord touched his heart, and as I was then no longer in France, they wrote me that he died with the most positive marks of salvation; he had prepared for it, receiving the Sacraments very often, and having his confessor always beside him. The day of his death he fell on his knees in an intense transport of love of God, and expired in this position, leaving us, as I have said, sure marks of his salvation."

God revealed beforehand to Blessed Mother Anne of St. Bartholomew the time of her death. This is how it was known: A fervent novice, who, because of her health, could not remain at the Carmel of Valenciennes, came to tell her trouble to the Blessed Mother. Guided by a prophetic light, Anne of St. Bartholomew said to her "that at Ghent she would enter a monastery of another Order, to which God called her. She added: "I will still be living when you make your vows there, but I will live but a short time after that act." All was verified: the novice was received at Ghent in the monastery at Doriseé of the Order of Citeaux; her novitiate finished, she made her solemn profession there on the Feast of the Most Holy Trinity, the year 1626, at 10 o'clock in the morning, and on the same day, four hours later, as will be seen, Anne of St. Bartholomew left this exile.

We will close this chapter by the relation of a fact in which the prophetic light of the servant of God shone forth in a most touching manner. In the College of the Jesuits at Antwerp there dwelt a holy religious; a man of very high prayer and filled with zeal for the salvation of souls; he had great renown for sanctity in the city and throughout the whole country. This apostolic man, this son of St. Ignatius, was Father John Chailant. From the time of her arrival at Antwerp, Blessed Mother Anne of St. Bartholomew had had intimate relations with him, and her soul had received much light and great consolation from the words and direction of the man of God. On the day of the Feast of St. John the Evangelist, patron of the holy Jesuit, Anne of St. Bartholomew was in a profound ecstasy; in this ecstasy God revealed to her the sanctity of His servant, and was pleased to make known to her his wonderfully beautiful death. The holy religious was sitting in his cell, his hands raised to heaven, his face full of joy. The holy athlete of Christ, also seeing near him the seraphic virgin,

Life of Blessed Anne of St. Bartholomew

whose sanctity he understood, said to her with a look of happiness never to be forgotten: "St. John the Evangelist has just been here; he has given me the most consoling news possible for me to receive in this world—it is that at this very hour I must depart for heaven." Having said these words he took his flight to the heavenly country, in presence of the inseparable companion of St. Teresa. Having come out of the ecstasy, Anne of St. Bartholomew knew she could be certain that the holy Jesuit had left this exile at the hour and in the way she had seen.

It is sweet to us to recall by this account the memory of this apostolic man, and to attest the intimate relations which, from the beginning, existed between the daughters of St. Teresa at Antwerp and the Fathers of the Company of Jesus, for what the holy foundress, Blessed Mother Anne of St. Bartholomew established, should be kept up until the end.

CHAPTER VI

COMMENTARY

RENOWN FOR SANCTITY

This humble virgin never had any aspiration other than to serve God at Carmel and to be unknown in the world; but the more she humbled herself, and hid herself from the eyes of men, the more God made her known, and the more her heroic virtue and miracles made her celebrated throughout Christendom. Princes and kings never mentioned her name but with reverence. Philip II, King of Spain, held her in very great esteem and venerated her as a Saint. All the lords and ladies of his kingdom, following the example of their sovereign, thought it a great happiness to communicate with her by word or letter. Henry IV, King of France, his Queen, Marie de Medici, and all the nobility of the kingdom, considered her as an angel from heaven; and she was truly an angel in character and by the graciousness with which she gained the hearts of the French people.

Her renown was beyond belief; almost all the kings and Christian princes of Europe begged her to recommend them to God. The King of Spain wrote to her Highness, the Infanta Clara-Isabella-Eugenia, to take the greatest care of this religious, to whose prayers he believed he owed the preservation of the citadel of Antwerp. The Prince of Poland visited her and asked her for little pictures with her name written with her own hand, that he might give them to his father, the king, and to his brothers. During the conversation he was filled with so great reverence that he was unwilling to cover his head in her presence; it seemed to him there was about this virgin, nothwithstanding her poverty and humility, a certain majesty which obliged him to remain with head uncovered before her.

On a memorable occasion Paul V showed the esteem he felt for this Blessed Mother. He had been shown the documents of the process instituted for the canonization of St. Teresa; and though there were to be found there the depositions of persons high in secular and ecclesiastical dignity, learned and pious religious whose testimony had great weight and great authority, he said the testimony which pleased him most because of its depth and worth, was that of Mother Anne of St. Bartholomew, not only owing to the sanctity of the person, but also because of the Order, the arrangement, the clearness and admirable justice with which she recounted the virtues, actions and words of the holy Mother, whose disciple and companion she had been.

But among Christian princes, no one equaled her Serene Highness the Infanta Clara-Isabella-Eugenia, in her confidence in and

Life of Blessed Anne of St. Bartholomew

respect for Blessed Mother Anne of St. Bartholomew. Being in her country home at Marimont with the Archduke Albert when the Blessed Mother was on her way to found the Monastery at Antwerp, their Highnesses wished her to stop there, in order that they might see her and enjoy her holy company. The Archduke held a conversation with her first, and after that the Infanta never left her. They were both charmed with the sanctity which shone forth from her. After this interview their veneration for her person and their faith in her power with God were unlimited. The Infanta kept up an intimate correspondence with her. She consulted her regarding the most important affairs, and never undertook anything of moment, without having first recommended it to her prayers. She considered her one of the strongest defenses of her dominions. One of her ministers having one day represented to her the necessity of reinforcing the troops of the citadel and the city of Antwerp against the enemy, she replied: "I fear nothing for the citadel, nor for the city of Antwerp, for Anne of St. Bartholomew is there, and she alone is worth all the armies of the world."

When she was about to lay siege to Breda, she stopped at Antwerp, entered the convent three times, had long conversations with the servant of God, and humbly throwing herself on her knees before her, asked her blessing. She requested the Blessed Mother to come to the door of the cloister and bless the grandees of her court and the chief among the officers who were leaving for Breda. "Receive, sirs," she said to them, "the blessing of Anne of St. Bartholomew, which will be your safeguard and the pledge of your victory." All with bowed heads and bended knee received the blessing of the servant of God; and soon after the Catholics entered Breda as victors.

The renown of her sanctity spread through all Germany and the Northern countries. Catholic Poland, the country of Stanislaus and Sobieski, revered her as one of the holiest souls then in the world. Here are the terms in which the Primate of the Church of Poland wrote to this illustrious Spouse of Christ: "Blessed Virgin, consecrated to God; Mother and Sister dearly beloved in the Lord. We have blessed the God of heaven, that in this sorely tried century He has in your person manifested to the world a most brilliant torch of true piety and real sanctity, shedding its light in the Order of Carmel; and because He has exalted you by the gift of the richest and rarest ornaments of grace, as we have learned from our well-beloved and venerable Brother Andrew of Jesus. We will not fail to beg the Father of Mercy an increase of grace for you, and that He will favorably receive your prayers, to which I recommend my person, this kingdom, surrounded on all sides by fierce and barbarous nations, the king whom God has placed at its head, and the holy Catholic church whose ship is tossed about by the upheaval of such great wars. I beg of you, virgin consecrated to God, to remember Us in the prayers you offer Him daily. And may it please our Lord to preserve you for long years, most brilliant star of your holy Order, support and ornament of the Christian people.

"From Zesnena, this 26th of September, 1623.

"Your Father and servant in the God of your charity,

"LAURENCE,

"Archbishop, Primate of Poland."

While the Primate of Poland was writing with such veneration and confidence to the Blessed Mother Anne of St. Bartholomew, the general of the Polish troops also wrote a letter in terms of most lively faith and filial respect. He begged her to recommend to God the soldiers of Catholic Poland, and himself who marched at their head.

CHAPTER VII

COMMENTARY AND TEXT
PROTECTRESS OF ANTWERP

In 1622 and 1624 she prevented, by her prayers, the city of Antwerp from falling into the power of the Dutch, which caused her to receive the glorious title of Guardian and Liberatrix of Antwerp. Before placing before the reader the continued account of the Blessed Mother Anne of St. Bartholomew, it seems to us only just to speak of the immense difference between the Holland of that time and the Holland of today. At the beginning of the 17th century, Holland was still subject to the infatuation of heresy. The fanaticism of error exciting the political passions among this people, they committed excesses against the Catholic religion which impartial history has recorded, and of which we need not speak here.

But during the 19th century Holland underwent a change. Catholics formed a third of the population, and the return to union with the church was in most consoling numbers. The actual dissenters were of too noble sentiments and were too enlightened to share the violent hatred of other times. They sincerely respected the liberty of Catholics, and worked in union with them to establish the prosperity of their country on a solid basis. It is true to say the Catholic church is really free in Holland. No country has surpassed Holland in the generosity of its Peter's pence, and in the numbers of the defenders of the Papal States. The whole world knows today, and history will tell it to the most remote countries, that Holland sent 1,224 Zouaves to Rome, and that one single diocese, that of Harlem, counts in this number 669. Their feats of arms, their heroic bloodshed for Christ and His Church, will form the most beautiful page of the history of Holland during the nineteenth century. In all the records there will ever live the reply of the Zouaves of Holland to their sovereign, when he asked them: 'What would you do were I attacked?" "We would make for you a rampart of our bodies, and we would defend you as we defended Pius IX." It is said that at these words the monarch shed tears of tenderness: noble tears which did honor to the prince and the Catholic Church.

In one word, Holland, because of all she has done for Pius IX and the Church, has been honored with the admiration and sympathy of the Catholic world. As for us, we cannot doubt that in the plans of Providence, Holland, as well as England, is reserved for great destinies. When these two peoples will place at the service of the Church the grand qualities given them by God, they will wonderfully advance the spread of the Gospel in the world. Let us now listen to the account of Blessed Mother Anne of St. Bartholomew:

Commentary

Regarding these matters of the war, some things have occurred in my soul which are undeniable. The day on which Maurice Nassau, Prince of Orange, marched at the head of a great army with the fixed resolution of taking Antwerp, he placed most of his troops in many ships. The night was very serene and tranquil; he said to his followers with the most joyous air in the world: "We will see that there is no one but God or the devil who can cause the failure of my undertaking." He assured them that they would take Antwerp, and that they would return rich. But suddenly a great tempest arose and a very violent cold wind, which froze the water; and the ships with those aboard were instantly sunk. Maurice alone saved himself and with much difficulty, running the risk several times of drowning, struggling against the tempest, the water and the ice, in such wise that he was sorely wounded. From that day he had no health, and finally died in consequence of this mishap.

That very night, knowing nothing of the treachery of our enemies, I was seized about midnight with a great fear and I commenced to pray, my arms extended towards heaven, with great impetuosity of fervor. My arms becoming fatigued from being thus uplifted, I let them fall; it seemed to me that someone raised them again towards heaven and an unknown voice said: "It is not yet time to stop, keep them raised towards heaven." And I remained thus until near daybreak. I felt then that what I asked had been granted. And really, it was so.

On another occasion, having gone to bed and being already asleep, I was awakened by cries coming from the dormitory of the religious. These cries continued after my awakening; I called out and, two Sisters coming, I said to them: "Go through the cells, and see which of the religions is sick, for I hear cries." The two Sisters, after having made the visit, returned to say to me: "All the Sisters are sleeping, and there is no one sick." I then said: "Tell all to dress, and we will go before the Blessed Sacrament, for there must have been some treachery. It was our holy Mother herself, it seems, who wakened us." And we all went before the Most Holy Sacrament. I then said to our Lord: "I bring Thy servants to Thee here. May they ask Thee what I desire; for my part I can do nothing"; and I meant what I said; for it is the truth that I felt confused in our Lord's presence.

We remained a little time in prayer, and soon I felt, without seeing or hearing anyone, that we could retire. I forgot to say that at the same time I heard the cries, I also heard the signal calling to arms in the citadel. I looked through the windows to see if there were any lights in the fortress, for we could see it from our house. I did not perceive any light, all was dark. In spite of that, I felt that some danger threatened us.

A few days ago I awoke at two o'clock in the morning. A powerful emotion in my soul told me it was necessary to pray, which I did. But after some time, as I was weary, I went to bed again. It was useless. I had become the prey of an anxiety which

Life of Blessed Anne of St. Bartholomew

would allow me no repose. I recognized by this that our Lord willed that I should pray. I began then to pray, my hands raised towards heaven, experiencing a strong emotion which told me to plead for mercy. For two entire hours, from two o'clock to four, without consciousness of myself, and powerless to resist, I remained with hands raised to heaven and interiorly urged to ask for mercy. All the following day I was like one dead, my body bruised, as if it had been beaten with a stick. I knew not then what had happened; but they told me later that the heretics had attempted to take possession of the city by surprise, and that they had not been able to succeed.

EXTRACT

From the Chronicles of the Carmel of Antwerp—How Our Blessed Mother Was Chosen by God to Be the Protectress of This City of Antwerp, Before and After Her Death.

Among the privileges and advantages which make this great city one of the most important in the world, one of the most noteworthy is that of having possessed several great and holy persons, such as St. Eloi, St. Wilebroed, St. Norbert, St. Walburge and several others who honored it by their presence, some to preach the Gospel there, others to defeat the heretics, others to obtain by their holy prayers a shower of heavenly blessings; but not one remained here, all finished their course elsewhere. There was no other, as far as we have been able to learn, but our Blessed Mother Anne of St. Bartholomew, that great servant of God, worthy inheritor of the spirit of St. Teresa, who finished her days here and has left us her venerable body, as a precious relic, in order that we might realize that Divine Goodness had destined her from all eternity to be the protectress of this city during her life and after her death. Therefore, we can say that she was admirably associated in the work of all the Saints who preceded her: for if she did not preach the Gospel as an apostle, her sex not permitting her to preach in the church, she at least cast light into human hearts, attracting so many beautiful souls here to the practise of the evangelical counsels in the religious state, by the renouncement of worldly goods, by unceasing prayer, and by the practise of all the lessons that our divine Master has left us, even to the commanding us to become perfect as His heavenly Father is perfect.

We have already seen, and we shall see again, how she has drawn down a shower of heavenly blessings on this city, by the communicating of every kind of grace which the citizens declare have been received through her intercession. We shall now see how she vanquished, if not heresy by means of argument, at least the heretics by her powerful prayers, when in the strength of their arms they threatened to bring this city under their power and deprive it of the liberty of practising the Catholic faith.

Protectress of Antwerp

In the year 1622 the Prince of Orange provided a powerful army, with such ingenious weapons of war, that, seeing the wind in his favor, encouraged also by the assurance given him by the heretics of the city that he would meet with but slight resistance, he cried in a loud voice, so that all heard: "I am certain of victory; beyond doubt I will succeed in my undertaking; only God can frustrate it; I fear now no human power." He then continued his route. God inspired His servant to pray earnestly, which she did, commanding her daughters to join their prayers with hers as fervently as possible, telling them to plead with our Lord not to abandon His faithful ones, and to repeat it several times. Her zeal was redoubled at two o'clock in the morning, and she prayed with so much fervor that her body sank to the ground from weakness. Before five o'clock, Reverend Mother Teresa entered her cell; in seeing her the servant of God said: "My daughter, oh! I am so weary! I feel as though my body had been beaten; there has been some great treason, for it seems as if I had fought against a whole army, and when I wished to rest a little, not being able to do more, and I lowered my arms which I had raised to plead with my God, a voice cried to me: 'Still longer, longer, longer still!' I was all bathed in perspiration."

Afterwards she continued in prayer until she heard these words: "It is finished."

Two hours later they learned the effect of these earnest and ardent prayers, and that in proportion as the servant of God redoubled them, the waters were troubled and the wind changed, so that when the Prince of Orange reached a town called Presbos, a frightful tempest arose, and at the same time the cold became suddenly so intense they could not make use of the ropes on the ships, which were striking one against the other; soldiers perished with their horses; and their presumptions Prince considered himself happy to be able to escape; he who shortly before thought that no one could withstand his power, fled vanquished by the power of the prayers of a Saint. However, he did not profit by the lesson, since he wished to attempt it again in 1624.

He undertook to surprise this city by the citadel in which there was not a large garrison; and the enterprise was so well conducted that he approached with his army of 20,000 men as far as a village called Berchem, at the gates of Antwerp. About nine or ten o'clock in the evening, having learned the position of the Catholic army, he detached a body of 2,000 men, who went directly to the fortress, carrying with them small boats, scaling ladders and other warlike instruments; they left the other soldiers near by in order to be aided by them in case of need. Having detached four sections of the chain which held the counterscarp of the fortress, they by this means slipped into the ditch scaling ladders twenty-six feet long, and two pieces of wood of the same size used to slip noiselessly into the ditch two little boats in which were the engineers; these reached the other side of the ditch, having with them another scaling ladder and other wonderful instru-

107

ments to destroy the drawbridge. They thought the moment of victory had arrived, when our Venerable Mother, true rampart of the faith and of this city, heard pitiful cries in the dormitory and knew that it was our holy Mother St. Teresa warning her of some treachery, and that the city was in imminent danger of falling into the enemy's power. She obliged all her sisters to rise, and led them to the choir before the Most Blessed Sacrament, to pray. There our good Mother was heard frequently repeating these words: "My Lord, if I, because of my sins, am the cause of this outbreak, may I be cast into the sea like another Jonas and let me perish rather than so many others." During this time a furious tempest arose accompanied by great wind which prevented the enterprise of the enemy from succeeding. Moreover their soldiers were seized with extreme terror; and fear having taken possession of their army, they were discovered from the fortress, and took flight, leaving their boats, ladders and other instruments.

This miracle as well as the preceding one, after very close study, was verified and approved by Mgr. Malderus, Bishop of that place.

It was thus that God, in His great goodness, deigned to reward the zeal of His faithful servant for the defense and preservation of this city, when in great danger of destruction. It was also for its good and prosperity that the holy Prioress so often exhorted her daughters to offer their prayers, being of the opinion that since it provided them with bread it was just they should pay for it by their intercession with God. And as she possessed in a high degree the virtue of gratitude, it would be difficult to describe how she appreciated the least charity shown her; she impressed this also on the minds of her daughters, and they on every occasion, when this city has been in any need, have recourse to their Blessed Mother. At her tomb they plead with her earnestly to continue after her death the good she effected with so much zeal during her life, and their confidence has not been disappointed, as they have experienced on different occasions. As for the miraculous assistance that the inhabitants of this city receive every day from the mantle she wore, and a little earth taken from the place where her body rests, of that we will treat more fully elsewhere. They are, however, sufficient evidence of the truth announced at the beginning of this chapter, since by this means can be seen the care she still takes to protect and assist by her powerful intercession all the inhabitants of this city.

CHAPTER VIII

SHARE IN OUR LORD'S AGONY

In the Midst of a Great Interior Trial, Our Lord Gives Her the Assurance
That He Will Be With Her Until the Moment When He Will Conduct
Her to Heaven—Share in Our Lord's Abandonment on the Cross, and
in the Sufferings He Endured in Each of His Wounds, Until She Gave
Her Last Sigh.

During the war with Germany, our Lord gave me a great zeal
for the exaltation of the Church; it seemed to me my soul knew
no repose day or night. But the divine Master, who showed me
so much love at that time, suddenly hid Himself from me for
several days. My soul was as if alone in a desert, and in deepest
darkness. Moreover, I was disturbed by the fear that all the
favors I had received up to that time were only illusions. I resigned myself in all things to the will of God, but I experienced
a contraction of the heart, as if it was held in a press. This was
during the feasts of Christmas time, which I passed in a very
different state from that of other years. On the Epiphany, as I
was approaching the Holy Table fearfully, because of my want of
fervor, our Lord appeared to me most lovingly; before uniting
myself to Him in communion, I was filled with an impetuous attraction of love and deep recollection; and while receiving the
Sacred Host, the Adorable Master said to me: "I will be your
companion, until I take you with Me to heaven." My soul seemed
burning with love, and penetrated with reverence and gratitude
towards His divine Majesty, who had granted me so great a
grace and one which I had in no way merited. This vision and
this experience passed very quickly; but for several days I enjoyed the presence of God in a remarkable degree, together with
habitual peace and consolation, and an ardent desire to begin at
last to walk in the path of virtue, which I had never done until
then.

Now, I usually endure great sufferings in my soul, and have
done so for two or three years. They are so great, that had I
not known and enjoyed the goodness of our Lord, I might lose
confidence. But He has left me this grace: that no matter how
crushed I may be, I am always resigned to His will. This was
my disposition in the midst of the pain before this transport of
love of which I have just spoken. My soul suddenly saw itself
enveloped in a kind of cloud darker than the darkest night experienced by bodily eyes. But this cloud, though dark and full of
bitterness, is interior; and comes with such force that sometimes
it causes my hair to stand on end. The soul accepts it, however,
showing pleasure and very great resignation. Soon the cloud takes
entire possession of her. Under its influence, the soul seems dying,
she thinks she has reached the end of her life. She would not,

Life of Blessed Anne of St. Bartholomew

however, even if she could, be free from this agony. She prefers
to abandon herself entirely to this death, rather than resist it,
since it is more pleasing to God. I do not know how it is that this
so possesses all the powers of my soul, that I live as if I were
not alive. All is quiet and the soul free, without knowing how it
is so. For the pain is so interior, it seems I am in a strange
country, where one neither sees nor hears anything agreeable;
there is nothing but darkness everywhere, and the soul feels so
crushed, that it seems to be under a press. The one consolation
she enjoys is not to be inclined to pass lightly from one object
to another, as in other circumstances, and in other kinds of prayer;
she remains, on the contrary, firm in not wishing any diversion
which could cause her the least scruple. To die and leave her
exile would be her repose; but she does not ask it, neither does
she wish it; not the slightest inclination leads her to desire anything but the state of resignation in which she is. The divine
Master causes her to experience that abandonment of all things
He felt in this world, and particularly during the time of His
Sacred Passion. This sentiment and illumination by which He
revealed to me what He endured, is something so delicate that I
have no words to express it and no meditation can raise us to it,
if our Lord does not give us experience of it. And when this
sentiment passes, another comes no less real and no less magnificent; in this the divine Master allows the soul to realize the
intense suffering which He endured in all His wounds, until finally
He gave up His life in the midst of the abandonment of which I
have spoken; but He shows the soul that what gave Him the
deathblow on the Cross was love. When the soul reaches this
point, she can bear no more, and goes out of herself, saying:
"Lord, take my heart from me. I wish to be consumed and to
immolate myself entirely for Thee, and if this sacrifice of myself
is necessary that Thou mayest be more and more exalted in all
creatures, and that they may know Thee, ah, may I be entirely
consumed and immolated in Thee!"

I cannot tell in what way a soul who has this love and this
experience offers herself in the presence of her God, nor how she
says to Him: "Lord, if it is necessary for Thy glory, mayest Thou
be exalted, and I immolated and sacrificed." Truly, when love
reaches a certain point, it makes one mad, forgetful of one's self,
and has the effect of delirium, if it can be so expressed.

CHAPTER IX

VISIONS IN HER LAST HOURS

Grace by Which Our Lord Makes Known to Her the Abandonment She Will Suffer in This World, and the Sorrow and Contempt She Will Have to Endure—He Said to Her: "You see what I have suffered; well, all that is for you"—Excess of Love With Which These Words Inspire Her—Apparition of St. Teresa—Love Which the Saint Shows Her—Admirable Vision of the Most Holy Trinity in Her Soul—Apparition of the Blessed Virgin and St. Joseph—Ecstasy When It is Said to Her: "Your Spouse loves you dearly, and He suffers in seeing you suffer."

Some time after having received this proof of the love of my God, I once more fell into a great interior affliction, which was not less painful than the one I have first recorded. It lasted several days; and as my soul was disturbed with the fear that the graces I had received were only an illusion, I turned to prayer and commenced to consider the poverty and abandonment of Jesus Christ in this world, as well as the sufferings and contempt He had to endure. The divine Master showed it all to me in a light which I had never had before. It had never been granted me to penetrate these mysteries as I then did. I would like to be able to express or make known what was shown me then, but it is beyond my power. The divine Master revealed to me things so exalted that even if I passed my whole life reflecting on them, I could never find terms to express and make known what my Savior allowed me to experience at that time. My soul was in so great affliction that my strength would not have been able to bear the emotion, had not God come to my aid. The hour for Mass having arrived, I followed it; at the time for communion, I arose, but was obliged to make a great effort; at the moment when I approached to receive communion, I saw that our Lord was there crowned with thorns, and He said to me: "You see all I have suffered; well, all that was for you." I was as if out of myself, incapable of uttering one word. I then recalled those pronounced by St. Augustine: "Lord, if I was God, and Thou Augustine, I would become Augustine, in order that Thou mightest be God, so great is the love I bear Thee." I can truly say that this same love and sentiment animated my soul; and that the love which consumed me was excessive.

Several days when I was making the meditation, our holy Mother appeared to me, with the same countenance she had in life. She showed me much kindness and love, and this on three different occasions. My soul being in deep recollection, I made an effort to rouse myself from it. I opened my eyes, and saw that the holy Mother was there; she embraced me, and I returned the embrace; then she remained a few moments with me, and disappeared. I remained in deep recollection; and while in this state turned the eyes of my soul toward the good Jesus and His

Life of Blessed Anne of St. Bartholomew

holy Mother, who were in my heart, as I have said. Suddenly
I saw in spirit the Holy Ghost and the Eternal Father in great
Majesty; they were above Jesus Christ, as when they were present
at His baptism, which He received from the hands of St. John.

This vision was of very short duration, but my soul continued
so filled with God that, judging by what I felt, I could say with
St. Paul: "It is no longer I who live; it is Jesus Christ who
lives in me." Since that vision I have the happiness on certain
days, to enjoy this same presence of Jesus Christ our Lord and
that of His holy Mother.

Some time after this favor, one morning on awakening the
glorious St. Joseph placed before my eyes all the graces with
which God had favored me, thus showing me that I was more
and more obliged to tend to perfection.

On another occasion I was for three days in such darkness
and such agony of soul, I did not know where I was. On the
feast of St. Matthew of this year, 1624, I went to the choir in the
evening, and sat there, after having adored the Most Blessed
Sacrament as well as I could. As a ray of light penetrates through
the window of a dark room, so there entered into my soul a little
stream of light, and I heard it said to me: "Your Spouse loves
you very much, and it grieves Him to see you suffering." From
this little light, my soul was ravished in God; and entirely out of
herself she spoke in verse, expressing herself but with a slight
difference in the words of the Spouse in the Canticles:

> "Oh, Fount of Crystal!
> Oh, that on Thy silvered surface
> Thou wouldest mirror forth at once
> Those eyes desirable
> Which I have in my heart delineated!"
> —St. John of the Cross.

This satisfied and consoled my heart, which was as if famished
and fainting from weakness. For, in that state of obscurity from
which I had just emerged, nothing that I saw, nothing that came
to my mind, satisfied me. I could not even meditate, as I usually
do, for meditation consoles; and then nothing good entered my
soul. Blessed be this Adorable Savior, who cannot endure that
we should be in pain without consoling us, and who merits because of this that we should love Him with the purity He desires,
as He has shown me not long since.

CHAPTER X

COMMENTARY

REVELATIONS TO HER FRIEND CATHERINE

The Divine Master Appears to Catherine of Christ at St. Joseph's Monastery at Avila—Makes Known to Her the Interior Sufferings of Anne of St. Bartholomew, and Orders Her to Write to Her and Deliver His Messages—The Blessed Virgin and St. Teresa Appear to Her Also, and Give Her the Same Advice.

As we have seen, from the time of her arrival at Antwerp, Blessed Mother Anne of St. Bartholomew had been on Thabor because of the wealth of divine consolations. To be the true Spouse of Jesus crucified, she must experience Calvary with its abandonment and suffering. It was towards the last days of her life that it pleased God to complete her purification, by causing her to pass through the crucible and furnace of aridity, abandonment, and interior suffering. But while the divine Master shared His sufferings and abandonment on the Cross with His faithful servant, His love for her would not permit Him to see her deprived of all consolation. Sometimes He Himself spoke to her; and to pour balm on her interior crucifixion, a word like the following was sufficient: "I will be your Companion until I lead you to heaven." But then, when He hid Himself from her again, and allowed her to drink deeply of the chalice of His abandonment on the Cross, He ordered one of her friends at St. Joseph's at Avila to speak to her in His name. This friend was Catherine of Christ, one of the holiest souls of the Spanish Carmel. Born in 1565 at Villacastin, the birthplace of Isabel of the Angels, and Ribera, the historian of St. Teresa, she was from her cradle the object of the predilection of the divine Master. Her older sister, Mary of the Conception, had entered St. Joseph's of Avila; she would have wished to follow her, but she could purchase this happiness only by long combats. Finally, in 1592, at the age of twenty-eight years, she saw the doors of St. Joseph's open for her, and the following year, on the 20th of April, she made her profession as a lay-Sister, taking the name of Catherine of Christ. The divine Master led her in very exalted paths and showered favors upon her. Catherine of Christ was an angel of purity, and a prodigy of penance, a soul living only for the salvation of souls and the love of God; in one word worthy to be the friend of Anne of St. Bartholomew and to carry to her the messages of the divine Spouse. Having entered St. Joseph's of Avila twelve years before the departure of the Blessed Mother for France, she had during this interval the happiness of watching her, of being formed in her school, and of coming in contact with the furnace of divine charity which consumed her heart. A union was formed between them which was destined to be eternal. These ties, which

113

Life of Blessed Anne of St. Bartholomew

were so strong and so tender, were one day to aid the designs of God over Anne of St. Bartholomew. Therefore, when this virgin endured at Antwerp the sufferings we have related, our Lord appeared to His dear Catherine at Avila, and made known to her the interior crucifixion of her friend, telling her how pleasing her resignation was to Him, and what reward He had in reserve for her humility and patience. He commanded her to write to her, and repeat the very words she had just heard. Catherine of Christ hastened to make known to her friend the message of the divine Master:

"May the Holy Spirit, the spirit of fortitude, give you His love and consolation, Mother of my soul; to express and make known all my affection, and all my love for you would take too long; it is because you are so dear to me, that our Lord has appeared to me and made known to me your anguish and your sorrow. These are the words He has commanded me to repeat to you; may He speak them to you Himself, and you, my Reverend Mother, receive them as coming from His divine mouth, for it is to you all these words are addressed. 'My well-beloved daughter, cherished child, behold how much I love you and how dear you are to Me. Think that for love of you I came down to this world, and that My Father sent Me to drink a bitter chalice. From the day of My birth, I felt the cross. My holy flesh commenced to suffer, and I never more ceased during all My life by day or night to bear the cross; finally like a lamb, I allowed Myself to be led to the slaughter. I was in complete abandonment, deprived of My honor, of My beauty, of My dignity, of all consolation, and in tribulation such as no man ever knew. To My Apostles, who were My friends, I did this favor to give them My Cross, and they were maltreated as I was. As for My Mother, she had the greatest share in My sufferings; she was the Queen of Martyrs, her martyrdom having been incomparably beyond that of all others. I love My daughter Anne so much, that I wish to place her, through suffering, in the rank of My apostles. It is as a proof and mark of My love that I send her bitterness and sorrow; in the same manner that I tried Job on the dunghill, and as in the abandonment of his friends and the deepest sorrow the strength of his love shone forth most resplendently, so I try My daughter Anne; the greater the tribulations interior and exterior through which I cause her to pass, the more exalted will be the glory she will receive from My hands; and the more will the martyrdoms she suffers shine in the precious crown I have destined for her. When all is over, Anne, My daughter, I will honor you in heaven, I will seat you at My table, and will reward you for all you have suffered after My example in such great abandonment. And since by your prayers and your example, you honored Me on earth, I will honor you in heaven. I have great feasts in reserve for you there; and I will give you all that I possess, all that I enjoy. And what glory! it will have no end.'

Revelations to Her Friend Catherine

"Now, see, my very dear Mother, all that your most loving Spouse has charged me to say to you.

"CATHERINE OF CHRIST."

This letter was written; but before it left for Flanders, Catherine of Christ had another admirable vision. The most holy Mother of God and St. Teresa appeared to her and told her to write to Mother Anne of St. Bartholomew to make known to her how much they loved her, and they promised on their part the greatest favors. Catherine of Christ obeyed without delay and added this new letter to the preceding one: "When I went to prayer, after having written to you, the most holy Mother of God and our holy Mother Teresa appeared to me, giving me proofs of much love. They told me their love for you was very great, and they ordered me to make this known to you and to assure you that they would assist you in all your sufferings and tribulations; that they would be your most faithful Mothers until the end, giving you always the support of their favor and their consolation; that in the future life they will give you thousands of favors, and will receive you with open arms and with the greatest tenderness; that therefore you should take courage and be greatly consoled; that your pilgrimage will be well rewarded, and that the recompense will cause you to be inundated with joy." This is what the Mother of God and our holy Mother have told me.

"Another day, after Holy Communion, the divine Master told me that He was laboring to adorn your heart, and beautify it with the greatest virtues, that He would give you all He possessed in heaven, and that He would guard you; He added that He would Himself shine forth in your heart; thus giving you a grace above all other graces, and that He would protect all your religious; He told me that He reserved for you a martyr's crown; that without having shed your blood, you had been a martyr in your will, and that your life had been a long martyrdom; that He kept all written in letters of gold in His heart. All this comes from our good Jesus, and He has ordered me to write it to you. Adieu, my dear Mother."

The Blessed Mother received these letters at Antwerp, at a moment when she had reached the highest point of her interior sufferings. They dissipated the clouds which enveloped her soul, and restored its serenity.

The divine Master, as we shall see in the following chapter, revealed also to Catherine of Christ the circumstances of the death of Anne of St. Bartholomew, and the secrets of the great ecstasy which would precede it.

Catherine of Christ did not survive her holy friend more than one year; after having consoled her by sending her the messages of her divine Spouse, and after having in some sort written the last page of her life, she went to share her glory.

115

CHAPTER XI

COMMENTARY

HER GLORIOUS AND HOLY DEATH

Glorious and Holy Death of Blessed Mother Anne of St. Bartholomew.

We have now to describe one of the most beautiful and most holy deaths ever granted a Christian to witness.

God, who delights to return to His Saints glory for glory, willed that the marvels He caused to shine forth during the life of Anne of St. Bartholomew should be known to the Church. Eyewitnesses, the daughters themselves of the Foundress of the Carmel of Antwerp, made known some part of these wonders. The servant of God, by the words she addressed to her daughters, made known another part. Finally the divine Master revealed to Catherine of Christ, the holy friend of the saintly virgin, the secrets of her last ecstasy and of her entrance into heaven.

Therefore this death, in a cloister closed to creatures in a poor little cell, this death which must be, apparently, hidden in obscurity, was to be known to the whole world, and the account of it pass on to all future generations. Marvelous effect of the will and omnipotence of God!—this cell where Anne of St. Bartholomew died has become a public sanctuary for the whole universe, and it is granted all the members of the Catholic Church to look upon the sublime scene of this holy death; history permits us to assist at it.

Anne of St. Bartholomew had reached the seventy-sixth year of her age. From her tenderest years she had offered herself to God, she had consecrated to Him her virginity. She had lived more than half a century in Carmel. In Spain, she had the glory of following, as an inseparable companion, the holy Foundress in her final apostolic labors, and of holding her in her arms at her last hour.

France possessed her seven years, and God granted miraculous fruitfulness to the mission she filled there.

For fourteen years she seemed like another Teresa in the Carmel at Antwerp, the masterpiece and crown of all her works on earth. The divine love, whose fires her heart had felt from the earliest years of her life, never ceased increasing until the very end of her career; it had now reached the intensity of that of a seraph.

Apostolic zeal, the great virtue, the distinctive mark of Carmel, consumed her. Like the prophets and apostles, she had always been devoured by a holy zeal for the glory of God, for His church and for the salvation of souls.

The virtues practised in an heroic degree during so many long years had raised her to a height of sanctity known to God alone.

Her Glorious and Holy Death

As for the merits she acquired, and by which was to be prepared the crown destined for her by the just Judge, their immensity will not be known except in the light of heaven.

The austerities, the labors, sufferings from without, interior crucifixion from the hand of God, had made her life a long martyrdom.

By her purity, her zeal, her patience, she had merited the crown of virgins, of apostles and of martyrs.

Finally to describe in the words of the Holy Ghost Himself, so noble and holy a life, Anne flourished like the palm tree in the Church of God, and she was multiplied like the cedar of Libanus. This cedar covered, with its branches, Spain, France and the Netherlands.

How precious the death of this virgin was to be in the sight of the Lord! The day predestined for her entrance into heaven was the 7th of June, in the year 1626, feast of the Most Holy Trinity.

In her filial confidence, Anne of St. Bartholomew had asked of our Lord to die on this beautiful feast, and our Lord granted it to her. He did more. He revealed to her the year and the hour when He would call her to Himself. This much-desired hour was about to sound at last. During the three days which preceded the feast when all was to be consummated, the three divine Persons of the Most Holy Trinity were pleased to adorn the happy virgin for the eternal nuptials. Anne of St. Bartholomew, who already greeted the day of her deliverance, abandoned herself with transport into the hands of her God, and unceasingly responded with the most heroic fidelity to the gifts and favors of which she was the object.

The Thursday before the feast of the Most Holy Trinity, the divine Master visited His faithful servant towards evening, and shared with her what had been His most precious possession in this world, His cross. Anne of St. Bartholomew was suddenly seized with a fever which consumed her; the night was passed in this fire which was for her a sort of purgatory.

But in the morning, rising at the usual hour and overcoming the fire of the fever by the fire of divine love with which she was filled, she went to unite herself with Jesus Christ in Holy Communion.

Possessing the divine Guest and already leaning on Him to take the journey to heaven, she remained on her feet almost all day, notwithstanding the suffering and sickness she experienced. Towards five or six o'clock in the evening she made a general confession to the Prior of the Discalced Carmelites; the Lord so permitted, in order that they could have from her own mouth this memorable testimony: "By the grace of God," she said to her confessor, "I do not think I have ever offended God mortally during all my life."

On returning from the Oratory where she had made her confession, being in greater suffering, she went to bed towards seven o'clock in the evening. Then the divine Master, wishing to give her a new proof of His love, caused her to endure a part of the sor-

117

Life of Blessed Anne of St. Bartholomew

rows of His passion. She felt in her left shoulder one of the most dreadful pains that could be endured here below: it was as if the bones were dislocated and were leaving their place. This martyrdom lasted all the night from Friday to Saturday. Though she was an ocean of patience, she, however, ordered a Sister to touch her shoulder, pronouncing at the same time the name of Jesus. The religious were surprised that she had thus asked to be relieved, having always noticed, that no matter how great her sufferings, she never complained. They suspected there was something extraordinary in it. The heroic Spouse of a crucified God, keeping her secret, did not make known to her daughters the intensity of the martyrdom she had endured all that Friday night; she only asked the relief we have mentioned. But the day of the feast of the Most Holy Trinity, when towards midnight, as we are about to see, the divine Master imprinted upon her for the last time His Cross and His sufferings, the Blessed Mother said to a Sister: "My daughter, if in the suffering which I endured all Friday night, our Lord had not strengthened me, by making me understand that it was similar to what He Himself endured, when they stretched out His arms to nail Him to the Cross, I would undoubtedly have despaired and lost patience."

Thus the secret of her suffering was revealed. That Friday night she was on Calvary with her divine Master; she shared part of His crucifixion. All day Saturday she endured this great agony of suffering. The divine Master then lifted the cross, and poured oil on the wounds He had inflicted on His faithful servant. He renewed her fortitude, because in His love for her He would twice again place the same chalice of suffering to her lips. Saturday night, our dear lover of the Cross once more ascended Calvary: the Well-Beloved permitted her to be overwhelmed with suffering; she was consumed with fever, her other pains increased, and in her shoulder, which seemed dislocated, she felt the tortue experienced by her divine Savior when they stretched His sacred arms to nail them to the Cross. Crucified and inundated with happiness, ever ready by excess of suffering to give up her soul, and in a rapture of love at being able to share the cross of her well-Beloved, she united her sufferings to those of her Savior, her Spouse and her God. Thus passed the hours of this second night. Witnessing the excess of her sufferings, the Sisters who assisted her feared every moment she would expire in their arms. But this Saturday night was the last of her exile. The Cross was to reap for this faithful Spouse of a crucified God an immense harvest of merits: all that night angels adorned her crown, and each each moment of crucifixion, so lovingly borne, was a new diamond added to this crown.

The dawn of the longed-for day broke at last: it was the feast of the Most Holy Trinity. Anne of St. Bartholomew came down from the Cross, and the divine Persons commenced in the earliest hours of that great day to pour into the soul of this virgin, who was so dear to them, the first waves of that torrent of delights, at

Her Glorious and Holy Death

whose fountain-head a few hours hence their love would immerse her for all eternity. They rained down graces and favors upon her soul. They appeared to her in an intellectual vision, as they had done many times before, but now the veil which concealed the divine essence and the adorable mystery of the Most Holy Trinity became more transparent. And, as the Most Holy Trinity is all love, by communicating with this soul in a more intimate manner than ever in the past, they left it consumed with love. And, as the beauty of God appeared to her in a brighter light, she received a divine wound deeper than all that had preceded it. She was burning with such ardent love, so wounded, in such great ecstasy, the thought of the infinite felicity of God already weighed so heavily upon her, that the strength of her love would have a thousand times broken her bonds, if God had not by a miracle detained her here longer. But after these ecstasies, after these visions of the adorable mystery, foretaste of the clear vison and entire possession of God which was to succeed them in a few hours, Anne of St. Bartholomew could no longer contain within herself the great joy she experienced. She was as if transfigured; she was made as beautiful as an angel; that flower of eternal youth, unchanging gift of the inhabitants of paradise, shone from that countenance where suffering the two preceding nights had set its sign and seal. She conversed with some of her daughters regarding the mystery of the Adorable Trinity; but from her burning words, one would think a seraph spoke with her mouth. All that morning Anne of St. Bartholomew was as if inebriated with heavenly delights.

Towards midday the Most Holy Trinity was pleased to show His power, and to bestow with greater munificence than ever before the infinite treasure of His graces upon this well-beloved virgin. Wishing to raise her merits to a supreme height, in order that her glory might be the greater, He granted her yet more precious graces than those of ecstasies and inebriation with divine love. A third time Anne of St. Bartholomew felt herself fastened to the cross of her divine Master, and she endured the suffering or rather the crucifixion of which we have spoken. While she was a prey to this exquisite martyrdom, which completed her resemblance to her dear crucified Master, she asked them to place a relic of the holy Mother Teresa on her shoulder, to see if it would relieve her suffering. But Teresa, whose will was united to God's, Teresa whose motto was, "To suffer or to die," aided her in suffering and was careful not to lessen her merits by relieving her pain. Anne of St. Bartholomew, who knew the hour when God would call her, then sent a message to the Discalced Carmelite Fathers, begging each one to say an Ave Maria for her, and she asked her daughters to do the same. A change was soon visible in her countenance, and her condition announced the approaching end. The Carmelite Fathers arrived at the same moment as the physician; and realizing there was no longer any hope, they hastened to give her Extreme Unction. Before receiving it the Blessed Mother, who had lost the power of speech, but preserved full consciousness,

Life of Blessed Anne of St. Bartholomew

made with her own hand the sign of the cross on her mouth, and on her tongue, which had become stiff and motionless.

While she was receiving these sacred unctions, a miraculous change took place in her. Her countenance shone, her features, contracted by pain, became composed; the wrinkles of age disappeared; a supernatural beauty appeared on her face, transforming it, causing it to shine with a light infinitely more pure than the flower of youth. Suddenly the eyes of the seraphic virgin were raised on high towards the side of the wall, they beamed with indescribable brightness; they were fixed upon the divine object which had just appeared to them. Anne of St. Bartholomew contemplated what was revealed to her, with an ecstatic smile. This rapture lasted for the space of a quarter of an hour.

What passed then? The divine Master, while desiring that a solemn silence should accompany this vision, willed, however, that the great things which took place in these supreme moments should be known for all time in the Church. He, therefore, revealed all to the tender friend of the seraphic virgin, to Catherine of Christ, who was at St. Joseph's of Avila. And it was by favor of the narrative of this confidante of the divine Master that we can assist at all the marvels which took place during this last ecstasy.

The cell of Anne of St. Bartholomew presented a spectacle similar to that witnessed in Alba in Spain, the 4th of October, 1582, at nine o'clock in the evening, in the cell of the seraphic Teresa, when the divine Master, with His Mother, St. Joseph, the ten thousand martyrs and a numerous escort of angels, came to seek the soul of that virgin. The Saint, at that solemn moment, was leaning on the heart of her faithful companion, Anne of St. Bartholomew; she was encircled by her arms, she wished to pass from the arms of this angelic virgin to those of her Savior and her God. The divine Master, who willed at last to place the crown upon her head, revealed Himself to her soul in greater beauty than ever before, and with still greater love. This beauty and love gave to Teresa's soul a double wound which caused her death. And from the heart of Mother Anne of St. Bartholomew, her last support in this world, she passed to the heart of her God, there to rest during an eternity of centuries.

At Antwerp the scene of Alba was repeated, but with a something greater and still more solemn. The day on which Anne of St. Bartholomew was to enter triumphantly into heaven was the feast of the Most Holy Trinity. During that day, which is so holy, the entire heavenly Court unceasingly exalts this most Adorable Trinity, and no feast, even in heaven, is comparable to it. In the decrees of His ineffable love, the divine Trinity had chosen this solemnity to crown the companion of St. Teresa. Coming down from the heights of heaven and followed by the heavenly Court, He appeared to this happiest of virgins, revealing Himself to her in an intellectual vision. Therefore, Anne of St. Bartholomew contemplated in her ecstasy the three divine Persons of the Most Holy Trinity, and with them the heavenly Court which accompanied

Her Glorious and Holy Death

them. The divine Master was there before her eyes; the Immaculate Virgin was there, as well as St. Joseph; she looked down upon her with motherly eyes; the virgins surrounded her, prepared to be her guardians on her entrance into the glory of heaven; the Saints, men and women, all the blessed Spirits, regarded affectionately the one whom the Most Holy Trinity deigned to honor with such a weight of glory, and eagerly longed to have her with them in paradise. At last the divine Master spoke these words:

"My friend and My well-beloved, come, enjoy the palm of victory that you have merited by your patience, and by your perseverance in well-doing; the hour of labor has passed. Come, chosen Spouse, you have imitated Me to the very end, ever inviolably faithful to Me, and like a pillar in My Church, by your continual prayer and your rare humility. Enjoy now forever this eternal abode; you will be crowned with three crowns among the virgins and the martyrs."

At these words, Anne of St. Bartholomew, wounded like Teresa with a wound of love which killed her, took her flight and rose upward, following the Son of God, to her eternal home, accompanied by the canticles of the Saints and the heavenly Spirits. The three Crowns prepared by the Divine Spouse were placed upon her head, and the inseparable companion of the apostolic labors of St. Teresa is recognized throughout eternity as the inseparable companion of her glory. It is therefore at her side that she receives the acclamations of all heaven, and it is at her side that she celebrates with the whole heavenly Court this divine feast of the Most Holy Trinity; and henceforth she will, for an eternity of centuries, participate in the glory and felicity of her God.

But at the moment when the soul of this happy virgin took its flight towards heaven she bequeathed to her body, the faithful companion of her labors, a reflex of her glory, and imprinted upon it the eternal seal of sanctity. It remained in the attitude of ecstasy. The features wore the expression of rapture caused by the vision the soul had contemplated before leaving it. So wonderful a participation in the very majesty of God glorified this virginal body in such a way that one could not contemplate it without falling on their knees. A celestial perfume, an odor never known on earth, exaled from this body, which for 76 years had been the temple of the Holy Spirit, and which during eternity should be a thousand million times more resplendent than the sun. This perfume penetrated to the souls of those who had been witnesses of so holy a death, or rather of the commencement of a divine life. The greatly favored daughters of Anne of St. Bartholomew shed tears for their Mother, but tears which contained something akin to the joys of paradise. They kissed her feet and hands with all the tenderness of filial piety, and with most profound religious respect. They felt that henceforth they could claim their blessed Foundress and Mother in an incomparably more devoted manner than when she was still living. She saw them in God, loving them in Him, never ceasing to intercede with Him for those she had so much loved in this exile.

It was at her bedside the Carmelites of Antwerp finished celebrating the feast of the Most Holy Trinity. During the night they still kept guard over their beloved Mother and contemplated her dear countenance; they turned to profit those most precious hours by confiding to her their requests and their desires, begging her to assist them by her influence with God.

Happy the city where this pillar of faith was to remain standing until the day of judgment. Still more happy the monastery where this sanctity, brilliant as the sun, had terminated its career. Happy the city and the house which possessed the virginal body of this Spouse of Christ. Happy the families, who by their faith and devotion, during the tempest of the last century, saved the sacred remains of this virgin: the blessings of God will fall upon them from generation to generation.

CHAPTER XII

COMMENTARY

HER LAST OBSEQUIES

Funeral of the Blessed Mother Anne of St. Bartholomew.

A ray of the future transfiguration had already fallen, as we have said, on the mortal remains of the new inhabitant of heaven. At the time of that stupendous vision, when the three Persons of the Trinity with all the heavenly Court had appeared to the virgin lost in an ecstasy, her virginal body was seen to be clothed, illuminated by the divine glory, and it remained as if engulfed in this ocean of light and sanctity. The impress of divine glory had remained upon her features. The inseparable companion of the seraphic Teresa triumphed at her side in heaven. God, who had united them by such intimate ties, was pleased to show the might of His arm, to prove to the world how dear they both were to Him, and how He honored them in His kingdom. He renewed for Anne what He had done for Teresa: at the moment when Teresa, in the form of a dove, took her flight to heaven, her virginal body exhaled a perfume which penetrated the whole Monastery of Alba. When her inseparable companion flew to the arms of her God, all the Monastery of Antwerp was inundated with a heavenly odor. The two virgins, at the moment of their entrance into heavenly glory, were like queens seated on a triumphal car; and after their last sigh they preserved that majestic attitude: the peace of heaven, the bliss of heaven, the glory of heaven was visible on their countenances and their forms. God willed that the funeral of both virgins should be a veritable triumph.

On Monday the Carmelites of Antwerp carried the body of their holy Foundress to the choir, and placed it before the altar. As the news of her death had spread abroad, there was an immense gathering in the church. The Catholic people of Antwerp were untiringly contemplating the countenance of this virgin; they venerated her as a Saint; they recommended themselves to her; and all wished to have something which had touched her virginal remains. The first day, more than 20,000 chaplets or pictures touched this holy body. Following the example of the citizens of Antwerp, the people of the neighboring country hastened to see the Saint, to recommend themselves to her power in heaven, and to have some object of piety sanctified by touching her body. The Infanta Clara-Isabella-Eugenia, to prove the devotion she had always had for the servant of God, wished to possess her scapular. According to Enriquez, Brussels was depopulated; not only the lower classes, but the nobles and several princes and princesses, departed immediately to venerate this holy body before it was placed in the tomb.

123

Life of Blessed Anne of St. Bartholomew

God was pleased to confirm this devotion by a miracle. A young girl of Antwerp, Catherine Lykens, fell head foremost into a deep pit; the fall was so great that the physicians and surgeons declared the injury incurable and death near. Then, full of faith, Catherine's mother hastened to the Carmelite Church, threw herself before the body of Blessed Mother Anne of St. Bartholomew, and begged her to restore her daughter. She felt that the servant of God had interceded for her; she rose up, ran to her home, and found her daughter completely cured. The miraculous cure was soon known throughout the city and increased devotion to the servant of God.

Her funeral was celebrated with the greatest solemnity.

Until Tuesday the holy body was exposed to the gaze and veneration of the public. It was then enclosed in a coffin and placed near the choir grate. The religious therefore continued to have their holy Mother at their head when they were at prayer or when they chanted the divine praises; and the people, insatiable in their desire to kneel at this tomb, were only separated by the barrier of the grate from the powerful mediatrix who did not cease to make them realize the effects of her power with God.

CHAPTER XIII

COMMENTARY

Marvels Worked by the Blessed Mother After Her Death.

Our Lord was pleased to make the tomb of His servant glorious by the miraculous favors and cures obtained by the faithful.

Let us listen to the chronicler of the Carmel of Antwerp on this subject: "It is not our intention to enumerate here all the wonders God has worked, and continues working every day, through the intercession of our Venerable Mother; this would be to undertake an impossibility, since they are innumerable. It will suffice us to confirm what is known through all these provinces, that she has had the grace to perform miracles of so high an order, that there is no kind of sickness whose cure she has not obtained.

"After her death," continues the chronicler of Antwerp, "this grace of miracles became more conspicuous. What was granted only to her blessing was obtained now by means of anything of which she had made use. The people continue up to this time, coming to beg the prayers of our Venerable Mother; they ask to place delicate children on her tomb: they beg for some water taken from the little pitcher which she formerly used in the refectory; and while drinking this water several fever-stricken and other sick persons were cured. Her mantle works wonders. Through the efficacy of this mantle with which they covered themselves with great confidence, several women in labor, who were in danger of dying or of seeing their child deprived of baptism, had a happy delivery. In fine, there has been no instance of helping and consoling others where her charity has not appeared in a miraculous way."

The powerful influence of the Blessed Mother with God, and the grace of miracles with which He is pleased to favor her, has not ceased to shine forth brilliantly from the time of her death until our own days.

It is not within our compass to give an account of so many favors and cures obtained through the intercession and influence of the inseparable companion of St. Teresa. Among the innumerable facts which attest the power of Anne of St. Bartholomew with God, we will cite only one, the cure of Marie de Medici, Queen of France. Our reason for choosing this particular case is because this queen was in her time one of the greatest protectors of Carmel, and because her name is connected, as we will see, with the history of the Monastery of Antwerp. We will here borrow again the words of the chronicler of this monastery:

"The Queen Marie de Medici, of glorious memory, who had known and honored our Venerable Mother in France, during her

Life of Blessed Anne of St. Bartholomew

exile in the Netherlands, fell sick at Ghent, in the year 1633, and was seized by a burning fever which lasted forty-four days, with increased temperature every night and anxious restlessness, which drove away sleep. Her Highness, the Infanta, not satisfied with having the physicians of the queen and the family, sent for those of the King of France. But as the seriousness of the illness surpassed the power of their science, all these learned men found themselves helpless to save the queen. Then the Venerable Mother Eleanor of St. Bernard, true and faithful companion of our Saint, and at this time Prioress of the Carmel of Ghent, sent to the queen a mantle which she kept and honored, because she had seen the Venerable Mother Anne of St. Bartholomew wear it. At the same time, she begged her to have confidence in the merits of this great servant of God. The pious princess received this good advice with the best disposition; and having ordered that she should be covered with this relic, she felt the sickness increase to such a degree that she thought she was about to succumb. Addressing her maid of honor, she said: "Salvage, how is this? This miracle will take me to the other world." Madamoiselle Salvage replied: "Your majesty must have great confidence; for I have heard when the Saints wish to grant a cure the suffering increases at first." Shortly after, the queen fell asleep; and into so profound a sleep that it lasted three hours, at the end of which she cried out: "Salvage, I am cured!" And summoning the physicians who were in waiting, they found the queen free from all trace of fever, and her pulse so steady that they published the wonder. They did not oppose her wish to make it known in person; she rose immediately, and made several trips through the city, and let all see she had recovered perfect health. She wished also to give authentic testimony, signed by her hand, and stamped with her royal seal, which we preserve in the archives of our convent. Here is a faithful copy:

"Marie, by the grace of God, Queen of France and of Navarre: We wish to testify that, in the year one thousand, six hundred and thirty-three, and the fourteenth day of the month of June, while in the city of Ghent, having been tormented for forty-four days by a slow, continuous fever, with increased temperature at night and great restlessness, which deprived us of sleep, after having used all human means to recover health, we had recourse to the merits and prayers of the blessed Mother Anne of St. Bartholomew, whom we had known intimately in France, where, through our interest and pleading, she had come from Spain with Mother Anne of Jesus, and four other religious, to establish the first monasteries of her Order, and from there, passing to the Netherlands, died several years ago in the city of Antwerp, greatly revered for her sanctity; all of which we learned from several persons worthy of belief, and that God had worked miracles in favor of those who invoked her; having also been informed that the mantle she wore during life had restored to health many sick persons, we had the desire to cover ourself with it. This having been done during the octave of her decease, and at our hour of repose, we experienced extraordinary suffering in all parts of our body; but they were relieved, and followed by a sweet and peaceful sleep, during which the fever left us entirely. Which we, and the physicians who attended us, have decided should be attributed to the prayers of the blessed Mother Anne of St. Bartholomew and to the touch of her mantle. We make this declaration, that it may serve for the glory of God, and the honor of His Saints, and have willed to sign it with our own hand and stamp it with our seal. Done at Brussels, the twenty-sixth of June, one thousand, six hundred and thirty-three."

It was signed Marie, and below, Deslandes. At the side is the royal seal in red wax.

This pious princess was not satisfied with making this declaration, but to give a more striking proof of gratitude she made a vow to strive with all her power to obtain the beatification of her great benefactress, and she came to thank her at her tomb, offering her a shrine worth from eight to ten thousand francs, which is kept in the hope of placing her remains therein. The favor the queen Marie de Medici showed the monastery from that time cannot be expressed. She called the religious her daughters, and always gave them this glorious title, in their presence as well as in their absence. When God called her to enjoy the reward of her sufferings in the glory of heaven, she ordered in her will that her daughters of Antwerp should share the treasures of her Sacristy with the Carmelites of Cologne where she then was.

Pope Clement XII, as we have said in the Preface, issued in 1735 the decree in which he declared that Mother Anne of St. Bartholomew had practised the Christian virtues in a heroic degree. May it soon be followed by the decree of beatification!

LETTER

Of the Blessed Mother Anne of St. Bartholomew, to the Infanta Clara-Isabella-Eugenia. After the Capture of Breda.

(The original of this letter is preserved by the Carmelites of Antwerp.)

Jesus, may the grace and love of God be always in the soul of your highness. You must welcome the opportunity of taking a little repose. You, indeed, merit it after all you have done. Your servants and subjects of this monastery desire most ardently to see you. This letter is intended only to congratulate your highness on so great a victory. Truly, princess dear to my soul, what is seen every day shows plainly that you are another Elias; it seems as if God obeys you, and that He does all that your highness wills. Owing to the fullness of grace He grants you, I am not astonished it should be so. According to the testimony of the Hollanders, the Catholics have proclaimed even to the present moment that your highness prayed so continuously that by these petitions you achieved the victory over your enemies. As for them, they think your highness a sorceress. See what you have conquered by the graces God has bestowed upon you. These wretches know it well, but they will not give up; they remain obstinate, although they realize both your power and your mercy towards their compatriots who have fallen into your hands. Blessed be God who possesses so good a friend in these States, by whom He confounds them. May His Divine Majesty preserve her to us for many years. The desire of all here is that your highness will pass this way once more, and that it will be granted us to welcome you in this monastery where all is yours. We kneel humbly at the feet of your highness, offering you our most respectful greetings. We are in fairly good health, and always disposed to serve your highness. As Sister N—— is wiriting to your highness, I will now close, although it would be a great consolation for me to converse longer with your highness; this pleasure will be mine on some other occasion.

Your highness' unworthy servant,

ANNE OF ST. BARTHOLOMEW.

LETTER

Of Blessed Mother Anne of St. Bartholomew to Mother Eleanor of St. Bernard:

To My Very Dear Sister, Eleanor of St. Bernard:

Jesus, be with my very dear Sister. How distressed I am because of your ill-health, and how miserable my own is, because I cannot cure you. Truly, it is not from want of good will, nor because I have not recourse to God, begging Him to grant me the cure of so good a Sister. But, my Sister, how little power friends have when God wishes otherwise! May it then be so, and may His holy will be done. There is no friend like Him; if He works His will in us, it is for our eternal salvation. And, although I plead for your health in this world, I see that the will of your reverence is entirely conformed to that of your Adorable Master, which consoles me immensely. Another great consolation for me was the visit our Father made you; I think, my very dear Sister, this visit must have caused you very sensible joy. Please, on the first opportunity, express to our Father all my gratitude. Notwithstanding the pleasure it gives me to see him here, I do not desire it unless matters of necessity should bring him, as I fear the fatigue of the journey would do him harm. As for myself, I am getting on fairly well; the novices, as far as I can judge, are doing well; Mother Sub-Prioress is as usual, but she is well. I am under obligations to all. As they realize I am so good for nothing, our Lord gives them the desire to assist me. Louise acts like a capable woman; for, without absenting herself from the choir, she attends to the kitchen and has taken charge of the Turn. Please, my Sister, when you write to me, pay her a compliment, and recommend me earnestly to God; consider that I have great need of this in order to do all things well and that they may give pleasure to God. May He dwell in your soul, my Sister. I recommend myself fervently to the prayers of all your novices, and most particularly to my very dear Sisters Madeline of St. Joseph, Mary of Jesus, and Mary of the Presentation. I recommend myself last of all to the good Andreé; I have felt her sorrow deeply, but I will recommend her in a very particular way to God. I cannot converse with you longer, my Sister; I am in haste to finish.

Your Reverence's very little Sister and unworthy servant,

ANNE OF ST. BARTHOLOMEW.

(The original of this letter is preserved by the Carmelites of Orleans.)

H. S. Collins Printing Co.
St. Louis, Mo.

CPSIA information can be obtained
at www.ICGtesting.com
Printed in the USA
LVHW081301050520
655045LV00012B/217

9 780343 327859